TEENAGE COUPLES

CARING, COMMITMENT AND CHANGE

Other Books by Jeanne Warren Lindsay:

Teenage Couples—Coping with Reality: Dealing with Money,
In-Laws, Babies and Other Details of Daily Life
Teens Parenting—Your Baby's First Year
Teens Parenting—The Challenge of Toddlers
Teen Dads: Rights, Responsibilities and Joys
Do I Have a Daddy? A Story About a Single-Parent Child
School-Age Parents: Challenge of Three-Generation Living
Teenage Marriage: Coping with Reality
Teens Look at Marriage: Rainbows, Roles and Reality
Parents, Pregnant Teens and the Adoption Option
Pregnant Too Soon: Adoption Is an Option
Open Adoption: A Caring Option

By Jeanne Lindsay and Jean Brunelli:

Teens Parenting—Your Pregnancy and Newborn Journey
(Available in "regular" [RL 6],
Easier Reading [RL 3], and Spanish editions.)

By Jeanne Lindsay and Sally McCullough:

Teens Parenting—Discipline from Birth to Three

By Jeanne Lindsay and Sharon Rodine:

Teen Pregnancy Challenge, Book One:
Strategies for Change

Teen Pregnancy Challenge, Book Two:
Programs for Kids

By Jeanne Lindsay and Catherine Monserrat:

Adoption Awareness: A Guide for Teachers,
Counselors, Nurses and Caring Others

TEENAGE COUPLES
Caring, Commitment and Change

How to Build a Relationship That Lasts

Jeanne Warren Lindsay, MA, CFCS

Morning
Glory
Press

Buena Park, California

Teenage Couples—Caring, Commitment and Change:
How to Build a Relationship that Lasts
is part of a two-book series. The other title is
Teenage Couples—Coping with Reality:
Dealing with Money, In-Laws, Babies and Other Details of Daily Life

Library of Congress Cataloging-in-Publication Data
Lindsay, Jeanne Warren
    Teenage couples. Caring, commitment and change : how to build a
relationship that lasts / Jeanne Warren Lindsay
        p.   cm.
    Includes bibliographical references and index.
    ISBN 0-930934-92-X : $15.95. -- ISBN 0-930934-93-8 (pbk.) :
$9.95
    1. Man-woman relationships --Juvenile literature. 2. Teenagers--
Juvenile literature. 3. Love--Juvenile literature. 4. Mate selection--
Juvenile literature. [1. Man-woman relationships. 2. Mate selection.
3. Love.] I. Title. II. Title: Caring, commitment and change.
HQ801.L475 1995
646.7'7'8035--dc20   94-37983
                                                                CIP
                                                                 AC

MORNING GLORY PRESS, INC.
6595 San Haroldo Way   Buena Park, CA 90620-3748
(714) 828-1998
Printed and bound in the United States of America

CONTENTS

Teenage Couples—Caring, Commitment and Change: How to Build a Relationship that Lasts is the first in a two-book series for teens who already are married or living with a partner or plan to live with a partner at some future date. Suggestions are offered for building a relationship from choosing a partner to handling a possible break-up.

Sometimes a problem becomes easier to deal with if you know you aren't the only one with such a problem. Hearing someone else talk about feelings of jealousy, for example, may help you look more realistically at your own situation.

This book and its companion title, *Teenage Couples— Coping with Reality: Dealing with Money, In-Laws, Babies and Other Details of Daily Life,* are based on information, opinions, and suggestions from 80 young people I interviewed extensively. Each was living or had lived with a partner.

Thirty-one of the interviewees were married, and for 13 couples, both husband and wife were interviewed.

You will find many quotes from these young people in

these chapters. They talk about their realities as they struggle with lack of money, living with in-laws, extreme feelings of jealousy, and other problems. They also talk about the joys, the good things about their relationships.

Their comments have been edited slightly to mask their identities. Otherwise, all of the quotes in these books are real, and are taken from conversations with young people who were married or living together while still teenagers. Quotes were selected to illustrate concepts, but are strictly in the words of the young people.

Listening to young people talk about their realities as they struggle with relationships with partners may help you. If you aren't married or living with a partner, reading about the realities facing these young people may assist you with your future plans. The ideas presented for creative communication, money management, and on other topics can be useful whether or not you ever marry.

Mentioned occasionally are the results of the Marriage Expectations Survey. This survey was completed by 3,728 teenage men and women. The basic questionnaire (minus the biographical questions) is reproduced on pages 181-190, *Teenage Couples—Coping with Reality.* If you are in a relationship with someone, the two of you might find it helpful to complete this questionnaire—separately—then together discuss your responses. You each might gain valuable insight into the other's opinions and preferences.

How to plan a wedding is *not* discussed in this book. For many couples, their wedding provides happy memories and holds great symbolic value. However, a lovely wedding doesn't guarantee a good marriage.

If you're planning your wedding now, whether a big and elaborate or small and intimate ceremony, enjoy. If you want advice, you'll find excellent books on the subject at your local library.

Nurturing Your Relationship

If you're married or you're planning to move in with a partner, you've undoubtedly been told over and over of the difficulties bound to occur in teenage relationships. You've probably heard that more than 60 percent of teenage marriages fail within five years. But you know your relationship will be different.

Well, you can make yours different. You and your partner will need to work hard to keep your relationship going. Perhaps you already have several strikes against you. Maybe you have no money, you're living with his parents, and you have a baby you hadn't planned to have. It all sounds pretty difficult. But other couples in your situation have developed satisfying and caring relationships.

Developing a close relationship with another human being is one of life's greatest challenges. Achieving that close, loving and caring relationship is surely one of life's most satisfying experiences.

My hope is that *Teenage Couples* will help young people develop that satisfying and loving relationship.

Jeanne Warren Lindsay
November, 1994

Are teenage couples so different from older couples?
Few marriages are "made in heaven" and few couples
experience a stress-free relationship. Putting a male and a
female into close proximity with the expectation that each
one's life will be enhanced is an optimistic view. Much is
gained by having "someone always there for you," but
there may be a sense of loss as well. A good relationship
involves a lot of giving as well as taking, and for super-
independent or very private people, living with a mate can
be quite difficult whether you are a teen or an adult.

Teenage Couples—Caring, Commitment and Change
pulls no punches. It tells it like it is, right out of the mouths
of very young women and men who are either living
together or married. Teenagers on the brink of entering into
partnerships will benefit from learning about decision-
making, communication, romance, jealousy, dealing with
substance abuse and violence, and keeping it all going.

Teens today are confronted with so many don'ts . . .
don't smoke, don't drink, don't do drugs, don't have sex,

don't fail in school, don't feel sorry for yourself. It is refreshing to encounter Jeanne Lindsay's sage advice: Do find an appropriate partner, do get married if you are sure that it is feasible, do have fun and learn to enjoy each other.

Adults don't always have their acts together. As a wife, married to the same man for 45 years, I can attest to many of the points made in this book. If I were a young person, I would look first for someone with whom I had shared common interests. George, my husband, and I have always been absorbed by political processes. Our first conversation was about the 1948 presidential election (Truman won)! Our most recent discussion was about the 1996 election (will Clinton win?). We have not always agreed about politics or other issues, but we have remained respectful of each other's views. In the beginning of our marriage, I thought he didn't communicate enough, but later I was glad we didn't let "everything hang out" and maintained our independence and privacy.

I guess the key word is moderation, finding the right balance that keeps you on an even keel so you feel enhanced by the relationship but never smothered. There is no magic formula for a happy relationship. Couples have very different styles of relating to each other. If George had ever yelled at me, I would have been despondent. One couple we know, married as long as we, always communicate loudly and stridently . . . they claim it is their method of communication.

It is difficult to understand from the outside what goes on between two people. Sometimes a third party can help. Jeanne Lindsay's books are unique in that they provide direct suggestions about sources for counseling and treatment. Don't hesitate to seek assistance. The sooner you deal with a problem, the easier it will be to cope with it.

Another point is that you really do "marry" the other

person's family. When we married, George's mother was 70, old enough to be my grandmother. I figured she wouldn't be around long to interfere with our lives. She outwitted everyone and was just as mentally sharp at 92 when she died as when I first encountered her. As I matured, I learned to respect her enormously, and to understand the tremendous difficulties with which she coped in her own life. My son must have learned from watching us try to make Nana Lucy happy. Now that he is an adult, we are blessed with his and his wife's thoughtful and nurturing qualities.

My mother once told me that eventually generations reverse roles. The children become the caretakers of their parents. Children model their behavior on what happens at home, so the way that couples treat each other not only has an effect on them, it is carried over to the next generation. Violence begets violence. Caring begets caring.

Having children definitely alters the options for teenage couples. The delicate little life they bring into the world has to be fed, clothed, intensely loved . . . parents have to learn patience, generosity, sensitivity. Many teenagers lack nurturing parents themselves, and finding themselves parents, have to start from scratch, finding role models outside of their families, locating programs that can teach them parenting skills, and overcoming significant economic and social barriers. Teen parents have to understand that hanging out and partying must take second place to home responsibilities.

If I may add one final word of advice (another don't), don't squander your teenage years. Unless you are really prepared to assume all the responsibilities that go with partnerships, living together, early marriage, and early parenthood, wait. Have fun, learn, grow, gain experience, prepare yourself for the future. If you want to find out if you are ready for taking on a partner and a family, *Teenage Couples—Caring, Commitment and Change* will be your guide. If you know that you are ready, this book will enhance your life, learning how other young people overcome barriers and strengthen their relationships.

Joy G. Dryfoos
Author, *Adolescents at Risk: Prevalence and Prevention;*
        Full Service Schools: A Revolution in Health and
                Social Services for Children, Youth and Families
Hastings-on-Hudson, New York

ACKNOWLEDGMENTS

Many, many teenagers have helped with this book. More than 3,700 completed the Marriage Expectations Survey which is mentioned in several chapters. Results of this survey provided valuable information concerning today's teens' thinking on the topics of marriage and living together. The survey was administered by nearly 100 teachers across the United States, and I appreciate their willingness to participate.

Most of all, I appreciate the teenagers I interviewed in depth. All of these young people had lived or were living with a partner at the time of the interview. Without their insight, their willingness to share their problems, their frustrations, their joys, and their techniques for building a strong relationship, this book would not have been written.

To protect the anonymity of the interviewees, their names have been changed in the quotes, but many of them gave me permission to list their real names here. They include Anna Plum, Lester Bravo, Aimee King, Alyssa Levocz, Amy Bustria, Ashley Harrison, Brandi Rubio, Cheryl Crump, Christi and Chris Coen, Kristine Sharits, Christine and

Raymond Teachey, Christy Boynton, Cynthia Alvarez, Delia Arellano, Diana Arroyo, Donnell Gaines, Doreen and Rudy Rodriguez, Emelina Rosario, Erin and Mark Braaten, Priscilla Correa, Gabriel Garcia, Gabby Barcena, Gwen Godinez, Isabel and Aaron Goss, Jacqueline and Augusta Dawson, Jamie Baker, Jennifer Platz, Jennifer Rader, Jerome Sheridan, Nikki Hill, Joy and Louis Dixon, Kelly Marsh, Leticia Mendez, Lisa Stoops, Lora Stantz, Mandy Johnson, Jesse James, Maria Tongko, Mayra Raygoza, Michelle Pack, Michelle Rico, Travell Dupard, Michelle and Fred Oberst, Niki and Adrian Ghafoor, Niki Roschewski, Wayne Allen Saul, Jr., Rosie Vargas, Carlos Villa, Ruth and Isaac Guiza, Michelle Guilliatt, Marisol and Armando Barrozo, Tino and Donna Delgadillo, Tisha Brown, Jason Beard, Tammy Stratman, Wendy and John Monroe, Yvette Ireland, Julio Gutierrez, and Monica Quintero.

David Crawford's photos add a great deal to these books. Several people read the manuscripts and made helpful suggestions. These included Sol Gordon, Sally McCullough, Eugenie Wheeler, Judy and David Peterson, Trish Schlichting, Pati Lindsay, Erin Lindsay, Peggy Soule, and Lois Gatchell. I especially appreciated comments from Jennifer Oakes, 17.

I thank Joy Dryfoos and Susan Wilson for taking time from their busy lives to write the lovely Forewords for the *Teenage Couples* books. I admire and like them both.

Tim Rinker designed the covers, and Steve Lindsay oversaw the general design of the books. Carole Blum and Karen Blake helped with proof-reading and the many other tasks involved in the research and production of both books.

I especially thank Bob, my love, for his constant support throughout the researching, interviewing, and writing the *Teenage Couples* books, and especially for the forever relationship we have developed over the years.

Jeanne Lindsay

To Bob, my love.
Thank you for our forever partnership.

Are you ready for a forever relationship?

CHAPTER 1

Caring, Commitment and Change

*Older people often look down on teens in love.
Maybe they call it puppy love, but I believe in it. I
believe two teens can be very, very much in love. If
you aren't, I wouldn't gamble and start a family. I
wouldn't rush into a marriage without completely
knowing a person, knowing yourself and what you
want, then go from there.*

*If you don't know yourself, and you don't know
what you want, there's no way you can take on a wife
and a child.*

Johnny Angel, 19/Davina, 19 (Valizette, 11 days)

If you want to have a relationship that lasts, caring,
commitment, and change are key words.

- **Caring** is an important part of loving. Caring means
  you value your partner's welfare as much as you do

your own. You want to please your partner, and you
will work to build a satisfying, loving relationship
together.

* **Commitment** means you'll work through whatever
  happens in your lives and continue to care for each
  other.

* **Change** is inevitable, and a committed couple will
  grow and love through the changes that occur throughout their lives.

These are important concepts to consider as you choose
a partner. Some people suggest that ideally you'd date only
people you think could fill your needs as a life partner, but
that's not terribly realistic. It might make better sense to
suggest you *not* date people you know would *not* be good
partnership material over time.

So often today we see teenage parents struggling with
the belief that their child needs both parents, yet the parents
have very little in common with each other, or they don't
like each other any more. Instead of going on with one's
life and forgetting that short-term love, the young person
must deal with the parenting issue, a very big issue indeed.
Johnny Angel touched on this risk:

> *I feel if a relationship is serious enough to have
> intimacy, it should also be serious enough to think
> ahead. Frankly, if the individual is not somebody you
> want to be with in the future, you shouldn't make a
> bond by having a child.*
>
> *A lot of times the younger teens think it's all fun
> and games. It's not when you have another little life
> at stake. She is the casualty of the fun and games,
> especially if the other parent is somebody you really
> don't care about and you don't want to stay together.
> What's to happen to that child?*
>
> Johnny Angel

Falling in Love

Have you "fallen in love"? If so, you're probably excited and thrilled to be with your loved one. You'd like to be together constantly and forever.

Some people, however, feel falling in love has little to do with "real" love. It's a separate thing, sometimes almost a kind of blindness that says, "I have to be with this person."

"Growing into love" is a better foundation
for a good relationship
than is simply "falling in love."

Real love requires trust, respect and caring. When you fall in love, the early excitement may fade. But if, in addition to falling in love, you trust, respect and care for the other person, you'll continue to love. Friendship is an important part of a good relationship.

"Growing into love" is a better foundation for a good relationship than is simply "falling in love." With what kind of person do you think you could best grow into love?

If you and your partner share some of the same interests, that's a plus. If you can talk and be open with each other, that's a plus. If you argue, fight, disagree on almost everything, that's a minus—even if you're madly in love!

Luckily, a happy relationship doesn't depend on a special type of person. Outgoing fun-loving people always on the go can be happily married. So can people who want to sit home most of the time, including people who prefer an evening with a good book instead of in the company of a television set. The secret is for two partners to have interests which, if not the same, at least complement each other.

Opposites may attract, but if they have nothing in common, the attraction may not last long. It's possible for a

quiet person to enjoy being with someone who talks to
everybody and who is always the life of the party. Over the
years this might not be a happy situation.

*Juan doesn't like to go out and do things. Some-
times it makes me want to find somebody who does.
We can't talk about it because he gets mad. It depends on the mood he's in. I try to explain that it's
because I'm so young. "You don't like to do these
things, and that's not my fault. I want to go out."
Sometimes we go to the movies and maybe to the
mall. I like to shop, and once in awhile he will. Sometimes he won't even go with me to my family things.*

Angela, 16/Juan, 18 (Vaneza, 7 months)

Before you marry or decide to live with each other, learn
as much as you possibly can about your partner. Learning
later you don't like to do the same things could be
a disaster.

What Are Your Expectations?

*Today one of my friends at school said, "I'm
thinking about getting married. What do you think?"
I said, "It's real, real hard. Before you get married, discuss the ground rules. What's right for him
and for you? Discuss the 50-50—what's good for the
goose is good for the gander. Men like to dominate
their women. You stay home, cook, take care of the
children, don't talk back. Is that what you want?*

Karina, 16/Vincent, 20 (Saulo, 7 months)

What about your expectations of how a husband and
wife should act? Do you have about the same ideas on such
issues as who does what around the house, parenting
expectations, and money management goals? Do you agree
on what you expect of each other? Or does one of you

Marriage takes lots of caring and commitment.

expect the man to earn the money and the woman to do all the housework and child care while the other would like a more equal arrangement?

You need to talk about various kinds of expectations. First, do you have similar values? Do you agree on the importance (or unimportance) of education? Is one of you more concerned about thinking in the future while the other tends to be present-oriented? For example, you might want to plan and sacrifice now so you can buy that home of your dreams. Your partner may put higher priority on enjoying life today.

Looking for Commitment

Commitment means valuing each other's goals and understanding the importance of mutual support for those goals. It means working through the problems together and continuing to love each other.

The majority of teen marriages end in divorce. Undoubtedly the rate of break-up of teen living-together arrangements is even higher. So does commitment matter? If you
want a forever relationship, it matters a lot.

Later in this book we mention the six-month rule as a
technique for lessening the chances of break-up. If either of
you wants out, stall on your decision for six months. In
many cases, the problem leading to break-up may be solved
by then.

On another side of the commitment issue, however, is
the relationship that is truly bad for one or both partners.
Chapters 9 and 10 discuss some situations that simply
aren't good for people. Alcoholism, drug addiction, and
other big problems can be treated effectively. However, if
the addicted individual refuses to get help, there may be no
way the couple can have a good relationship.

Abuse is a huge issue in many women's lives. Too often,
the woman feels she deserves the abuse and/or she feels she
has no choice except to stay in the relationship. For an
appalling number of women in the United States, the
relationship ends in her murder by her partner. The tragic
situation of partner abuse is discussed in chapter 10, and
chapter 11 deals with ending a marriage. Some relationships, sadly, should not be continued.

If your relationship is a healthy, loving, caring partnership, however, commitment is important to both of you.

Change Happens

Change is a big deal in a relationship. On my 27th
wedding anniversary, I mentioned the event to a few
students. One young woman looked at me in amazement,
and said, "Twenty-seven years?! How could anyone stand
one man for 27 years?"

I explained that we have each changed so much over the

years that we each feel we've been married to several different people. It hasn't been boring. We all change a lot. The key is to continue to like your partner through these changes, and for your partner to continue to love you as you change through the years.

The catch in such changes over time
is that people may change
in different directions.

Those changes are going on right now. What were you like a year ago? Ask your partner the same question. Chances are you'll find some pretty big changes in both of you in that short time.

The catch in such changes over time is that people may change in different directions. "He's not at all like he was when I married him." "She doesn't seem to care anymore." Rapid change in the partner requires extra work and extra loving to keep a relationship strong and caring.

Already feeling those changes, Elijah and Janita demonstrate commitment and caring in their marriage:

We've been married five months. There have been a lot of changes, a lot of responsibility. I lived with my mom for 19 years in the same house, and moving out was hard. It was hard to get used to living away from home.

I'm working and paying the bills by myself because Janita's pregnant and can't work. If I get all stressed out, there's nothing I can do for her and the baby.

We were dating for three years before we got married, and I feel real comfortable with her. I think that's why I love her so much. It feels like I've known her all my life.

Elijah, 19/Janita, 16

Teens Change Rapidly

People usually change faster during their teenage years
than they ever will again. Do you sometimes feel very
mature, and at other times like a child? Are you feeling
independent most of the time lately, but at times you want
someone to take care of you? These are normal feelings,
especially among teenagers.

Such normal feelings, however, can make one a bit hard
to live with. Your mother may be able to cope when, as she
says, "You're acting like a child." But how will your
partner react to such behavior?

*At first you have good times. You move in, and it's
all good and nice and you like it. Then after awhile
you regret it, and you think, why did I move in if this
is all it's going to be? And you both feel all miserable
because all you do is argue.*

*Sometimes you get regrets. You see each other
every day and you don't really have much to talk
about. You start to nag each other about the littlest
things. There's nothing you can do. You can't get
away from her.*

Daesun, 20/Summer, 15 (Cecelia, 9 months)

If you have a baby, you may find it doubly hard. Many
young women find they grow up fast during pregnancy.
Sometimes their mates don't mature as quickly. "I feel like
I have two babies," a young wife commented. Sometimes
it's the man who, as he works hard to support his family,
matures rapidly. His partner, he feels, doesn't understand
the value of money and how hard it is to make the money
stretch to cover their bills.

Being patient with each other is important. Encouraging
each other to be the best person each of you can be will
help. Time will help—as each of you grows older, you will

probably grow more mature. It takes lots of self-discipline and lots of adjustment to learn to live with another person. If either or both of you are teenagers, it may take extra effort from both of you. But you can do it if you both work hard at succeeding together.

> *We've been living together for a long time, ever since Alexis was four or five months old. I was 14.*
>
> *Everything changes once somebody moves in. You get to know how they are, and you can't hide anything any more. I think we got closer, and we learned how to work together and take care of the baby.*
>
> *When Brandon goes out with his friends, I keep the baby. He does the same when I go out. I just have to let him know ahead so he can make plans.*
>
> Heather, 15/Brandon, 20 (Alexis, 13 months)

Change within a relationship is inevitable. Some change is good, some not so good. It's important to be able to adapt well to change. Otherwise, if the partners in their changing go in different directions, their relationship may suffer.

Much of the secret to changing together lies in good communication. If two people who love and care for each other can talk together about the changes going on in their lives, they can continue to grow together. They may find thirty years from now that each is an entirely different person—but that their love for each other has grown even stronger and more caring through these changes.

Two people working toward this goal are likely to be winners in the search for a loving, caring, long-lasting relationship.

*Choosing a lifetime partner
is probably the most important decision you will ever make.*

CHAPTER 2

Choosing
A Partner

Don't select him just because of his looks or his sex appeal. Jeremy and I talked about our goals and what we wanted to do when we got out of college. We had a lot of things in common. That was important.

Marlene, 16/Jeremy, 19 (Amber Marie, 7 months)

Living together is a big responsibility. You have to really know a person because it gets difficult living with somebody. The way you like things set up, the way you like things cooked, whatever. It takes a lot of patience and acceptance.

I think teens should really get to know the person before they decide to move in. They need to spend quality time together so they can get to know each other real close.

Zaid, 22/Tameka, 17 (Chantilly, 6 months)

Forever is a long time. You can have some control over your forever by making a good decision before you marry or move in with someone.

So how do you choose a partner?

Similar Interests Help

Do you and your partner share some of the same interests? Your relationship is more likely to be satisfying to both of you if you like doing some of the same things.

Some couples like to spend most of their time together. Others need time to pursue their own interests. Neither way is right or wrong. The important thing is for both partners to agree on this issue. If they do, either way of thinking and acting can be the basis for a satisfying marriage.

Will you work through disappointments and disagreements to make your relationship a deeply satisfying experience?

It is important that each of you has interests of your own. Relying on another person for everything doesn't usually work well. If you have some separate activities, you'll find you have more to talk about when you're together.

The list of things to consider in choosing a partner could go on endlessly, and you'll never find two people who agree perfectly on everything (unless one is a good liar). At least know where you differ before you commit yourself to a relationship which, hopefully, will continue throughout your life.

It's important that you both be determined to succeed in your relationship. Will both of you work through disappointments and disagreements to make your relationship a deeply satisfying experience for both of you? If so, you'll be closer to achieving a "forever" partnership.

Look for "Personality Fit"

Notice how your partner interacts with your friends and your family. Sometimes a young couple gets along wonderfully when they're alone. When they're with friends or family, however, one or both may find the other "acts different."

If you feel uncomfortable when you and your partner are with other people, try to figure out reasons for your feelings. Hopefully, you will work it out before you marry or move in together. Forever is a long time to be uncomfortable when you and your spouse are with other people.

Does your partner have ways of feeling and acting, of *being,* that you do or would like if you were living together? Do your ways of acting and being please your partner? Some people call this *personality fit.*

If you're "in love," you're likely to say "Yes" to these questions. Common sense tells us we usually like being with the person we love.

But think ahead to how you may feel about your partner several years from now. Will that charming fun-loving relaxed attitude she has still be as charming if she's so relaxed she doesn't find and keep a good job—yet you need two paychecks to survive? Will his admirable habit of always looking and dressing beautifully still be as admirable if there isn't enough money to pay for the clothes he buys?

What About Children?

Do you agree on whether or not you want to have children? Many couples today are delaying pregnancy until each has a chance to get a strong career going. Other couples decide never to have children. Others want several children right away.

A satisfying life is possible with or without children. The problem starts when one of you wants a baby and the other one doesn't. Or perhaps you have one child and you would like another, but your partner says one is enough.

If you want children, have you discussed child care? Not only how the work and joys will be divided, but *how* you want to raise your kids. If one of you "knows" children have to be spanked in order to become civilized while the other one says firmly, "People are not for hitting," how will you cope?

Have you discussed how you feel about the importance of work and career versus time spent with your family? Is one of you ambitious and expects to work very hard to get ahead while the other thinks it's more important to spend time at home? You may have trouble because of these differences.

Different Families, Different Cultures

- Do you and your partner belong to the same ethnic group?
- Are your family backgrounds similar?
- Is your religious faith about the same as your partner's?

Some happily-married couples grew up in very different family situations. However, couples with similar backgrounds tend to have fewer problems over the years.

If you decide to marry someone from a different ethnic group and/or religion, your parents may disapprove. You and your partner may need to compromise on a number of issues. But it certainly can work if the partners are truly committed.

In many parts of the country today, interracial relationships are more acceptable than they were twenty years ago. The couple involved may anticipate no problems caused by their different family backgrounds. Sometimes their parents are not as quick, however, to accept the situation. Danielle and Jordan discussed their

An interracial relationship may take some special caring.

life together and their family's reactions to their
partnership:

> *In the beginning, my family wouldn't talk to me.*
> *Jordan is black, and they didn't know I was going out*
> *with him until I told them I was pregnant. Then they*
> *kicked me out. That made it hard because in the*
> *beginning when Jordan and I had fights, I couldn't*
> *call my family—they weren't talking to me.*
>
> *Gradually it's getting better with my family. I*
> *missed my uncle a lot. I had two cousins, and they*
> *wouldn't let me talk with them. I hated it. But now the*
> *kids get along great with Jordan.*
>
> *There are some complications in interracial*
> *marriage, but I don't look for them. I think if you look*
> *for problems, you'll find them.*
>
> *If someone looks at me funny, I ignore it because*
> *they aren't living my life. One time we were stopped*

*by a cop and given a ticket—which they dropped
later. We knew it was because my husband was black,
I'm white, and his friend was Filipino.*

*It's hard. My family calls a mixed baby a half-
breed. I basically ignore it. My grandmother told me,
"If you have a baby, I'll love it no matter what color
it is."*

Danielle, 17/Jordan, 23

*My family had no problems with Danielle being
white. I resented her family when they didn't accept
me, and I'm tired of trying to make myself acceptable.
I figure if they can't accept me, they're missing out on
someone who could be a good friend.*

*Danielle's grandmother has always been nice to
me. Danielle's cousin didn't accept me, partly because I'm black, and partly because of my age.*

*Danielle missed her aunt and uncle and cousins a
lot, so I decided to lower my guard and see what
happens. So I talked with him. I said, "One of these
days maybe we can go out and shoot some pool."*

*"Let's let bygones be bygones," he said, and it's
been okay since.*

*It might have worked better if Danielle had
brought me into the family more slowly. Instead, I
never met her family until we told them she was
pregnant. If she had eased me in, her aunt and uncle
might have thought I was a nice guy.*

Jordan

Possibly the most important comment here is Jordan's "I
decided to lower my guard and see what happens." That
decision made all the difference in the relationship between
him and Danielle's family. Someone had to take the first
step, and for some people, that's difficult.

Another important piece of advice from Jordan was the idea that "easing him in" might have worked better than simply confronting Danielle's family with the fact that she was pregnant by a man of a different race. Families sometimes do better when they have a little time to consider and adjust to their realities.

Different family backgrounds and belief systems are at least as likely as racial differences to cause problems. If he grew up in a traditional household and she didn't, problems are likely to happen:

> *Justin is Hispanic and I'm white, and that caused clashes, basically because of his mother's bias. He came into the relationship with some beliefs about how I was supposed to be because of the way he was raised.*
>
> *He always thought he was the head of the household. So when our relationship came, basically I was in charge of Jameka and the housework, and he was in charge of working.*
>
> Meghan, 18/Justin, 21 (Jameka, 2½ years)

It's important that you and your partner be fully aware of these kinds of belief differences. How will you each deal with the differences? Discuss these things thoroughly *before* you decide to get married or live together.

If you agree that you fully accept each other's family, and intend to grow into caring and love for both families. you'll have a better chance of success in your relationship. Each of you may need to make some adjustments in your life style as you adjust to the other's culture.

This is often true, of course, for couples who appear to come from very similar backgrounds. Understanding and acceptance of other ways of living and being are important for all of us.

Possible Problem Areas

Do you and your partner argue a lot? If your answer is
"No, never," you're likely to have as many problems as the
couple who argues too much. Never arguing may mean one
of you is in charge and the other is going along with whatever that person suggests. That's not good for either one
of you.

On the other hand, if you and your partner argue constantly, how do you feel about continuing your relationship? A lifetime of fighting doesn't sound like much fun.

*Our arguing makes it hard for me to think we'd be
together forever. If we're going to constantly argue,
that's no good. I think if we communicated more than
we do now, we probably would stop arguing. The
arguing is getting worse as time goes on.*

Summer, 15/Daesun, 20 (Cecelia, 9 months)

Does either of you think the other one has a drug or
alcohol problem? The effects of overuse of drugs and/or
alcohol have ruined many relationships. Your wedding
won't change the situation.

What about jealousy? Trust is an important factor in a
good marriage. If your partner is upset if you look at or talk
to another person of the opposite sex, trust appears to be
lacking. See chapter 7 for a discussion of jealousy.

Is either your father or your partner's father into hitting
his wife? An alarmingly high percentage of men whose
fathers were violent are violent themselves. Women who
grew up seeing their mothers beaten tend to accept that
kind of life for themselves.

If your partner has ever hit you, consider it a red flag for
danger. Women, especially, because a woman is much
more likely to be seriously hurt if her partner hits her, need
to *stay away* from men who hit.

Perils of Dependency

The person who doesn't have high self-esteem may have a hard time forming a close relationship with someone else. High self-esteem on the part of both partners provides a wonderful foundation for a marriage.

Sometimes partners who don't have much self-esteem are overly dependent on each other. Neither thinks s/he can make it without the other. Sometimes it's only one partner who is not prepared to cope alone.

If either of you is depending on the other for most of your happiness, your relationship is not likely to work well. Neither is it likely to work well if either of you is overly dependent on the other for financial support or the day to day tasks of home-keeping and parenting.

If you are a man who follows the old ideas of the woman cooking and cleaning, and you don't know how to do these things, you have a dependency that will be a problem if your partner gets sick or no longer is with you.

A woman who feels she must depend on her partner for financial support can get in big trouble if her partner loses his job, is injured or killed, or the relationship fails.

For the best possible relationship, for the best chance of coping with whatever realities your life may bring, each of you needs to become as capable a human being as possible. Each of you needs to continue your education, obtain job skills, learn how to manage money well, know how to cook and keep house, and, if you have children, be able to parent those children well.

Many of us don't want to be alone, and that's fine. Being in a loving, caring relationship is a goal many of us have. That wonderful relationship, however, is much more likely to happen if it's between two self-confident people, each of whom would not starve to death alone. They are together *because they want to be.* That's what this book is all about—building that caring, loving relationship.

*You two have lots of things to consider
before you marry or live together.*

CHAPTER **3**

Making
the Decision

*Don't rush into a situation because of circum-
stances. Be honest with yourself and don't move in or
get married just to satisfy everybody around you.
Know for yourself whether you really want to share
your lives. When you're living together, all the secrets
come out, the money, breath, the snarling, everything
comes out. So be honest with yourself.*

Maurice, 21/Mitzuko, 16 (Lana, 14 months)

*My family wouldn't agree on my moving in with
Karina if we weren't married, and I actually wanted
to get married. I wanted my son to grow up with the
parents being married.*

*Sometimes, when we get in fights, I stop and think,
if I could go back, I should never have gotten
married.*

In a marriage there are some good things and bad things. I would like it to last forever. I'd like us to try to solve the problems and make it last. It's not only her and me. It's the baby, too. I see babies growing up with separated parents, and they get in trouble.

I see marriage as a commitment. If I feel like dropping it, I stop and think about it. Just deal with it and go forward, and don't quit.

Vincent, 20/Karina, 16 (Saulo, 7 months)

I lived with Jacari's father for a year. We split up because of a family fight.

I've been with my current boyfriend for 14 months, and we haven't even talked about living together. Ricardo is 19. He lives with his dad. I want to live with him because he's so much different, he's real mellow and he has a real good future, but I think I'd rather wait until we got married.

I've thought about moving in with him. That's what I'd like to do, but I think back and I think it's more fun this way. We see each other. He comes over to visit me or we go out. But when I lived with James, we didn't have time for each other. I just had time to take care of the house.

Angelica, 18 (Jacari, 3 years)

For many young people, the teenage years are a time to learn, to plan for their future. Friends are an important part of many teens' lives, friends of both sexes. Marrying or moving in with a partner too soon can be difficult.

What About Marriage?

A generation or two ago, many teens followed the pattern of dating, falling in love, and marrying. In 1950, about one in 6 teens married before turning 20. By 1980, it was one in 12. Today that percentage is even lower. The

median age at marriage today for men is 26, and for
women, 24. This means only half the men are married by
age 26, and half the women, by age 24.

Part of this change is due to more couples living together
before they get married. Of the 80 teens interviewed for
this book, 31 were married. The others were (or had been)
living together.

The suggestions here for developing a lasting relationship apply to couples living together whether or not they
are married. If you're not yet living with a partner, you'll
find guidance here for developing a better relationship
when you're ready.

For some people, living together before marriage is
acceptable. For others, it's not. Of the 3,800 teens responding to the Marriage Expectations Survey, four in five said it
was either okay (56 percent) or okay *if* they plan to marry
(25 percent).

Some people think living together may help prepare
them for marriage. Others feel they can learn enough about
each other through dating with no need or desire for a
living-together period. For others, the choice doesn't exist.
They simply feel living together without marriage is wrong.

My mom and Joe's parents didn't believe in living
together without being married. I don't think it would
be right for us. I think it's so much excitement when
you first get married and you have never lived to-
gether. I have a friend who got married after living
together for five months, and I don't see how they find
the excitement.

I think it would be easier to break away if you
aren't married. Your whole family goes to your
wedding. Then they're supportive, and they want you
to work things out.

Erin Kathleen, 18/Joe, 21

Moving in together would probably be a bad decision if either of you thinks it isn't right to do so. One of you may want to get married while the other thinks simply living together would be better. If this is so, you disagree on a very basic issue, and you would be wise to postpone both marriage and living together for awhile.

The Question of When

When "should" a young couple get married or move in together? Is there a "right" age? Is there a sure way to measure your readiness and your partner's readiness for living together?

How do you decide when or even if you'll get married or live with a partner? Is this something you're thinking about because you aren't happy at home? That's not a good reason to move in with a partner.

Angelica, quoted on the preceding page, moved in with James early in her pregnancy, She no longer lives with him, and she commented:

I moved in with James when I was 15 and he was 16. I was pregnant. It was different, and I felt uncomfortable. I had always lived with my mom, and here I was with new people.

In a way, it was fun. At that age I thought, hey, I get to live with my boyfriend. Yes, at first it was fun. Then it wasn't fun no more. He started thinking he wanted to be out with his friends but I couldn't go out with my friends because I had a big stomach. Then we started to fight.

Angelica

Of course, there is no magic ruler which will measure a specific couple's chance of being happy and satisfied with each other for the rest of their lives. Each couple must decide whether *they* are ready to commit themselves to each other. If you aren't already married, this book may help you decide if, when, and with whom you want to spend your life.

There's no rush to live together. If you think you'll be together that long, why rush into it? Wait until you're married and you have your career before you start living together.

Every time you argue, you can't say, "Move out." It doesn't work that way.

You may not think so, but living together changes everything. You don't have the freedom you had. You have more responsibility to him and to keeping the house. You have to be an adult, you have an obligation to someone else. It's a big thing to take on. It's not easy at all.

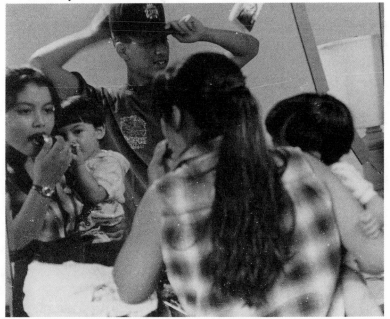

Privacy may vanish when you live with your partner.

> *You have to get along with him. You have to try to*
> *make it work. Every time you argue, you can't say,*
> *"Move out." It just doesn't work that way.*
>
> Brenda, 17/Santos, 18 (Lydia, 4 months)

The Legal Issues

If you're younger than 18, the law may influence your decision about marriage. In California, if either partner is under 18, the couple may be married only if they have parental consent for the person(s) under 18, permission of the Superior Court, and proof of premarital counseling for both. Other states have different requirements. Call the office of your County Clerk for information or see your pastor, priest, or rabbi.

If you have a baby and you don't marry, the father as well as the mother of the baby has legal rights. If the mother is taking care of the baby, the father still has a right to spend time with his child—whether or not he's providing financial support. This is true *unless* his rights have been removed by court order.

Both parents are responsible for the financial support of their child, whether or not they marry.

Importance of Finishing High School

Have you and your partner both graduated from high school? If not, you may decide it's best to live separately until you do.

> *If you haven't finished high school,*
> *that may be a reason*
> *to postpone marriage and living together.*

Many married and/or pregnant teenagers drop out of school. For many years, teenagers who were either

pregnant or married (or both) were *expected* to leave
school. They weren't allowed to stay. That has changed.
It's now against the law for a school to drop a student, or
even insist she attend a special program, because of pregnancy, marriage, or parenthood.

Many, many young people still drop out of school when
they get married or when they become pregnant. Those
who don't drop out may find their attendance and their
grades drop as they take on the responsibilities of marriage
or living together and perhaps parenthood.

> *When I moved in with him, it was harder for me to
> go to school. It was harder because he hardly went to
> school and he'd say, "Stay here," and I would stay.*
>
> *He was locked up for a couple of weeks, and now
> his P.O. says he has to go to school. We're going to
> the same school now, and it's working better.*
>
> Trina, 16/Victor, 16 (Felipe, 3 months)

---

*If one has finished school, do you both
think it's important for the other to continue
working toward graduation?*

Young couples and young single mothers and fathers
who manage to stay in school, attend regularly, and graduate have a *much* better chance of getting and keeping good
jobs. According to research, they are less likely to have a
second baby before they're ready.

Both factors help prevent the lifetime of poverty faced
by so many young people who have their first child before
they finish school.

If you haven't finished high school, that may be a reason
for you and your partner to postpone marriage and living
together. It's hard to play the adult role of living with a

partner at the same time you're going to school with teens who don't have the responsibilities you do.

Even if you or your partner is pregnant, living together at this time may not be the best thing for you. If you're seriously considering living together, ask yourselves these questions:

- Do we agree on the importance of continuing school?

- If one of us has finished school, do we *both* think it's important for the other to continue working toward graduation?

- Will I/we be able to get to school on time every day even if we're living together?

- When will I/we complete homework assignments?

Should Pregnancy Mean Marriage?

Most people in our culture prefer that a couple marry before pregnancy begins. But what if she gets pregnant before they're married? In the past, this usually meant a "shotgun" wedding. Parents often pushed for a quick wedding "to make it right."

A quick wedding doesn't necessarily make it right if you consider marriage a life-long commitment. Too often, these early marriages ended in divorce.

Only 8 percent of the teenagers in the survey said a pregnant high school-age couple "absolutely" should get married. An additional 7 percent thought this couple probably should marry. The rest felt it was important to base a marriage on choice rather than force.

It would have been a whole lot better if this had happened later. I'd rather have married him without being pregnant. Having the baby was like an excuse to marry him instead of a reason.

Karina, 16/Vincent, 20 (Saulo, 7 months)

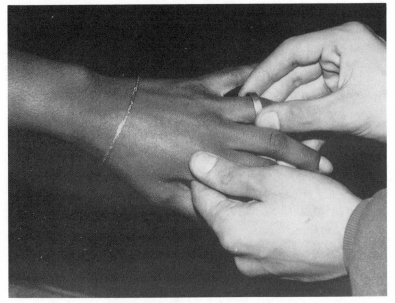

Should pregnancy mean marriage?

Sandra and Troy married early in her pregnancy, but Sandra cautions against a quick decision:

> *People ask me all the time, "You're married?" and they're like "Oh, that's so cool. I want to get married." I tell them it's harder than anybody thinks it is. I don't know why they want to get married.*
>
> *People think, "I can get married and get out of my mom's house"—but you have to get your electricity going, your rent paid, and it's especially hard when you have a baby. People try to take the easy way, and there's no easy way out. There are a lot more responsibilities than they think they're going to have.*
>
> Sandra, 18/Troy, 21 (Violet, 16 weeks)

If either of you should feel later that you have given up a lot because of your marriage, you're likely to blame each other. Being blamed for your spouse never finishing high school would be rough. "If we hadn't married I would have. . ." is often a painful thought. Before rushing into early marriage, both partners need to feel sure neither will blame the other for lost opportunities.

> *My dad said marriage is like an airplane. When you jump out, you can't get back in. "Do everything you want to do before you get married," he said.*
>
> *One thing I wanted to do was jump out of an airplane, so it was a weird example for me. I can never do that now because I have too many responsibilities. I would have loved to take a motorcycle and ride around the U.S. But I chose Erin Kathleen over that.*
>
> *There's too much you should do before you get married. When you get married, you have the rest of your life for that.*
>
> Joe, 21/Erin Kathleen, 18

Freedom and Friends

Before you and your partner start living together, consider carefully that you are likely to have less freedom to "do your thing" if you live with a partner.

> *Angela takes up a lot of my time. I'm still young, and I still like hanging around with my friends. But she always wanted me around.*
>
> *Even though she lived with us, she wasn't close to my family yet. She wanted me to be there while she adjusted to them. That caught me off guard, having to stay home a lot when she first moved in. I was kind of carefree before.*
>
> Juan, 18/Angela, 16 (Vaneza, 7 months)

Over time, some people adapt pretty well to the changes that come with living with a partner. For some, it takes time to adjust to a roommate, to share one's life with a partner:

At first, after Myra moved in, when I'd go away from here, it would be my getaway from Myra, and I kind of liked it. But now I'm used to having her here, and I like it now. Before, I felt kind of trapped. I changed because I love Myra. She's having my child and I want her to stay with me.

Sam, 18/Myra, 17

You can be sure of one thing. Living together causes changes in one's life.

No More Privacy

We never really knew each other before he moved in. Before, he would go home at night and I'd be here by myself. After he moved in, it was like, "Oh god, get out of my house. You're bothering me."

Shannon, 17/Steve, 17 (Koary, 4 months)

When a couple starts living together, one or both may feel they have lost an important sense of privacy. Sharing a room with a sister or brother is quite different from sharing it with a partner. You two may have tried to spend every possible minute together prior to the moving-in. Perhaps you just couldn't see enough of each other. Then suddenly, you're living together:

When he moved in, it was awkward. I wasn't used to having a male in our home. It was very awkward, confusing. I didn't have my privacy.
Now we pretty much share everything although we each have our own space at certain times during the day.

Anita, 18/Jarrod, 25 (Jarrod, Jr., 4 months)

Having your own space is important. If your home is crowded, this may be hard. Talk about it with your partner, preferably *before* you start living together. Try to work out a plan satisfying to both of you.

If One Is Older

Is your partner several years older than you are? Often, if the wife is very young when she marries a man a few years older, she plays a very dependent role. At first, both she and her husband think he should be in charge. As she matures, she may tire of this little-girl role. Sometimes the man can't handle it when his formerly dependent wife develops a mind of her own. And of course the reverse can happen if the man is younger or less mature than the woman.

> *I met Kent when I was 15. To me he was like, wow! older, probably smarter than me. But now it seems like I've outgrown him, and sometimes I regret that. But at the time it seemed so good.*
>
> *He wants to be with me all the time. He says, "I don't get to spend much time with you. You're always at school, and I want to be with you and the baby." I understand, but life goes on.*
>
> *Kent doesn't understand responsibility. I have to go to school, take care of the baby, clean our room, do the laundry.*
>
> Stephanie, 18/Kent, 20 (Satira, 8 months)

Maurice feels Mitzuko's age is a problem for him because she can't go where he wants to go, and he doesn't want to attend her school activities.

> *Our biggest problem is that Mitzuko finds fun in going to football games and to high school dances, and I already did those things. I go to them now and they're just dumb.*

I want to go places I can go because I'm 21. My best friend is 29. I don't think Mitzuko understands that I need to experience these things—like bars, movies we can't get in because of her age. The theaters card me and she doesn't have the ID, so we have to go see something else.

Like the prom—we had a real big misunderstanding about the prom. I'll be almost 22 when she has her prom, and I don't feel like going there. All those people are so young.

Maurice

Here's another place for compromise. Perhaps Maurice will decide to attend school events with Mitzuko simply to please her. In return, she may encourage Maurice to go out occasionally with his older friend.

Does Marriage Mean Control?

Sometimes one person, whatever his/her age, feels marriage means control. More often it's the male who has this "I'm-in-control" idea:

Marriage puts a new twist on the relationship. It's like, I guess, more togetherness, and I figure if we're married, we'll be together forever. Marriage would give me more control. We're still living in my parents' house so how much control is a different story. We never really discuss it.

Juan

If either of you thinks marriage would "give you more control," you need to discuss this idea thoroughly. A good marriage is *not* based on control. It's based on sharing, cooperating, and working together. If you have reason to believe your partner wants to be in charge as if you were a child, you may decide that's not the right person for you.

Don't Rush Marriage

Marrying or moving in with someone soon after you meet is risky. If you haven't had time to know each other well, you won't know whether your personalities "fit." It will be difficult for either of you to know what to expect of the other in your relationship. And in a brief whirlwind courtship, it is impossible really to know how much each is willing to sacrifice in order for the relationship to succeed.

Once you and your partner decide to get married or start living together, it's wise to wait awhile longer. Some experts recommend an engagement period of six months to a year. Instead of simply *falling* into love, you have a chance to *grow* into love.

> *Make sure you're together for at least a couple of years before you live together. A lot of things could go wrong. If she's not pregnant and things are going fine, keep it that way. Try not to bring the baby into it too quickly because it's hard. It's a real challenge to your relationship. Some of the guys feel they don't really need to deal with it because they aren't married to her and they can leave. So the girl gets stuck with the baby and it's hard.*
>
> *Babies should have both parents, all the time.*
>
> Davina, 19/Johnny Angel, 19 (Valizette, 11 days)

Some churches and social agencies offer premarital counseling. They often begin with a premarital inventory or other psychological test which can help you analyze your strengths as a couple—and areas of potential conflict. It's a good starting place for discussion and negotiation of topics you may need to discuss.

Churches usually do not charge for counseling. Social agencies usually have a sliding scale so that you pay only what you can afford.

What About the Dollars?

Finally, another very important question for you and your partner: Does either or both of you have a job that provides enough money to meet your expenses? Two *cannot* live as cheaply as one!

> *There's no way it could work. You can't rely on your parents when you're married. They're there for you, but you should definitely have a job. Keeping a job is a sign of responsibility, and you need that responsibility to stay married.*
>
> Erin Kathleen

For more about the expenses of marriage and living together, see *Teenage Couples: Coping with Reality*.

On pages 187-189 you'll find a "Scorecard for Predicting Success of Teenage Marriage." If you're thinking of getting married or living together, sit down with your partner and "test" your chances of having a successful relationship. If your score is low, you may decide to wait awhile before you marry or move in with your partner.

If you're already married or living together and you find your score is not as high as you'd like, treat it as a sign that you and your partner need to work especially hard at making your relationship succeed. Good luck!

Good communication between partners is important.

CHAPTER 4

Communicating with Your Partner

My most important advice is to communicate with each other. Share your thoughts. I'm learning slowly. I'm learning not to hide my feelings. I'm learning that he won't disappear if I tell him something he doesn't want to hear. He's very easy to talk to. He'll sit and listen.

Tiffany, 18/Shaun, 19 (Keosha, 11 months)

When we argue, we get real upset with each other, but we've never broken up. If you talk about it, you can work through anything with anybody. If you want to be with that person, you should be able to talk to him. If you can't talk, what kind of a relationship is that?

Sometimes Maurice and I have gotten to a point where we agree to disagree. We agree to honor each

other's opinions. Sometimes I don't like how he feels
about something, but I can't change it. So what's the
point of arguing if you don't get anywhere?

We try never to go to bed mad at each other. If we
can't figure out something in one day, it just doesn't
get figured out—until the next time.

Mitzuko, 16/Maurice, 21 (Lana, 14 months)

Nearly every young couple I talked with stressed the
importance of good communication in a relationship. Over
and over they said, "You've got to talk things out. You've
got to share your feelings."

Importance of Feed-Back

We talk a lot although I don't express my feelings
real clearly.

One night Janita said I married her because her
mom made me. I said yes and no. It was partly true
because her mom said, "I'm going to send her back to
Mexico if you don't marry her."

I said, "Okay, I guess we have to get married."

Then on the other hand, I wanted to be there with
my kid. I wanted to get married, but not now. Every-
thing was a little bit rushed.

That night it was really bothering Janita, and it's
good that we talked. I think communication is the best
way to keep a relationship going.

Elijah, 19/Janita, 16 (pregnant)

Sharing reasons for getting married is a big discussion
topic. Elijah and Janita needed to hear each others' feelings
on this subject. As Elijah's story illustrates, one of the big
breakdowns in communication often happens during the
receiving. One person says one thing and the other hears
something else.

At first, Janita heard, "I wouldn't have married you if your mom hadn't insisted." Because they talked, she understands Elijah's feelings more clearly. She knows he truly wanted to marry her, even though he might have preferred to delay their marriage until later.

Life is made up of little events and decisions as well as big ones. The little ones can cause problems, too. A question as simple as "What's for dinner?" could mean several different things: "Is dinner ready or shall I go to the bathroom first?" or "I'm starving—let's eat."

The person receiving the "What's for dinner?" message might hear something entirely different: "You must not be very efficient if dinner isn't ready yet" or "I hope we're not having tuna casserole again."

Simple feedback could be, "You're afraid we're having tuna casserole again?" or "I feel you're being critical because dinner isn't ready." This gives the other person an opportunity either to agree or to send the message again, perhaps in a different way.

Mixed Messages Cause Problems

Lance, 20, a perceptive young man, spoke of his concern with the mixed messages he was receiving from Peggy, 19. They've been married a year and, even though they both speak English, they aren't understanding each other:

> I think the exciting thing about going to a marriage counselor must be having someone sitting there listening to us both, then translating what we say into the other's language.
>
> For example, a friend of mine recently drove our car to the store for some beer. He'd been drinking a little, and he almost had an accident here in front of our house. We were lucky—he pulled out of it in time.
>
> When Peggy brought it up later, I thought she was

attacking me, saying my friend was stupid and shouldn't ever be allowed to drive. That wasn't what she said, but that's what I heard.

I realize now she was saying, "We worked hard for that car, and we need it to get to work. If it's wrecked, we have a big problem. Let's don't loan it to him again."

It was a big hassle. Instead of taking comments like this personally, I need to find a way to under-stand her more clearly. I guess I could have listened better.

Yes, Lance probably could have listened more carefully. Peggy perhaps could have chosen a better way to express herself. She might have said, "I feel worried when Tony drives our car because I don't think he's a safe driver." Lance could have replied, "I think you're worried about Tony driving our car."

If she agrees this is her "message," they can then discuss a solution. Perhaps in the future one of them will agree to drive Tony to the store. Or perhaps they'll set up a simple "No one else drives our car" rule. Whatever the solution, it should be easier to find once both partners understand the problem. The result could be one less hassle between Lance and Peggy.

If He Won't Talk

Communication is very much a problem. I sit there and beg him to tell me what he's thinking, and he won't. He sits there with his jaw set and he won't look at me. That really makes me mad. I know he hasn't learned to express himself, but I'm proud that he has opened up some. I guess just insisting and insisting on it will make it happen.

Karina, 16/Vincent, 20 (Saulo, 7 months)

Talking over the day's events can be a relationship-builder.

Several young people described silent mates, partners who refuse to discuss. In our culture, the male is likely to have a harder time expressing his feelings. From infancy, little girls are talked to more than boys. Girls are encouraged to show their feelings while boys are expected to "act like a man." Boys aren't supposed to cry. In fact, the "strong silent type" is often considered a positive label.

> *I try to wait until he's ready to talk to me. I can talk and yell and scream until I'm blue in the face and it won't work. We really don't talk and have conversations.*
>
> *We don't sit down and talk about anything important, like the baby or the car. At most, our conversations consist of "Yes," "No," and then I know he's listening to me.*

All I can say is just keep trying. If one wants
something and the other one wants something, and
their ideas or needs don't match, you have a problem.
                    Jillian, 17/Richard, 18 (Kevin, 15 months)

Is More Talking Always Better?

Certainly communication between partners is important.
But how much talking adds up to "good" communication?
The answer varies, of course, from person to person, couple
to couple.

Marvin Greenbaum, clinical psychologist in Portland,
Oregon, has an interesting viewpoint on the importance of
lots of talking between partners. "I think it's overvalued,"
he said bluntly. "Sometimes trying to communicate to your
partner *everything* you're feeling simply adds more
pressure to your relationship.

"Maybe it's like sex," he continued. "They say a couple
with a good sexual relationship considers sex about 25
percent of their total relationship. But if a couple has a
lousy time in bed, they think sex should be about 90
percent of the marriage.

"For many people, communication is a lot like that. If
you have it, it's not a big deal. But if you don't . . . that's
when the importance of communication may be over-
emphasized.

Remember that communication between people
can happen without words.

"A lot of young couples say you've got to be honest, you
must tell people how you feel. But this can have two
effects," Dr. Greenbaum explained. "First, it adds a lot of
pressure to their relationship. Second, there's an inequality
there because girls are generally better at communicating

than boys are. I see people expecting too much out of communication. Sure, it's an important part of marriage, but it doesn't offer a magic formula for happiness forever."

We need to remember that communication between people can happen without words. Lance explained:

> *Peggy wants to talk all the time. She thinks we're not sharing our lives if we don't talk about everything we do. I can sit on the porch with her beside me and read for two hours and feel close. She thinks we've got to talk or we're not communicating.*

Plan Time to Talk

Sometimes people won't talk because they don't think they have anything to offer. Or they may feel talking won't change anything so why bother? Often a person may be afraid to express feelings for fear of being rejected.

If your partner doesn't respond when you're ready to discuss a problem, think about how you communicate the rest of the time. Does your mate share feelings, dreams, frustrations with you? Would you like to talk more?

> *When I have a problem with Alfonso, I ask my mom, "What can I do to make him talk to me?" She tells me to talk to him and explain that I'd like to talk more. She offers to baby-sit Sylvia so we can go out somewhere and just talk to each other. She says that's one of our problems—we aren't spending enough time together.*
>
> *Sylvia is here, Alfonso is working, and I go to school. When he comes home, he's tired. He goes in the living room and crashes on the couch. The only day he gets off is Sunday, and he always just sleeps all day.*
>
> *Mom says to fix him breakfast in bed, and she will take the baby to church with her. We've done that a*

*couple of times, and it helps. It's hard to talk with
Sylvia here.*

Arlene, 14/Alfonso, 16 (Sylvia, 4 months)

Arlene's mom is offering valuable help. With Alfonso
working hard and coming home tired, no wonder he isn't
eager to talk a lot. Do they have dinner together when he
gets home? Or breakfast? If they can be alone together for
either meal, they can make that a time for sharing. Of
course baby Sylvia complicates things, but soon they'll be
able to feed her first, then let her play near them while
they talk.

Judson works 3 p.m.-midnight, and Aracely goes to
school all day. It's extremely hard for them to find a time to
communicate:

*I scarcely see him during the week, only on week-
end mornings. He calls me from work. Sometimes he
wakes me up for a few minutes to talk when he
comes home.*

*Keeping our relationship going is very hard. When
we're together, we just pick on each other. I'm usually more tired than he is. When he comes home, he's
wide awake. He wants to talk, and I just want to go
back to bed.*

*Chianti goes to bed whenever she wants, usually
after 9 p.m. She doesn't see her dad at all during
the week.*

Aracely, 18/Judson, 27 (Chianti, 18 months)

Spending time together is important in relationship-
building. How could Aracely and Judson find some time in
a schedule like this? There are possibilities.

If Aracely puts Chianti to bed regularly by 7 or 8 p.m.,
Aracely could get several hours rest before Judson gets
home. She might be ready to talk awhile when he shows

up—especially if she's able to get back to sleep easily.

Or perhaps Judson could get up and have breakfast with Aracely before she goes to school. If they plan a no-rush hour in the morning, they may find they enjoy their time together.

If you and your partner have a similar schedule, look at the whole 24 hours. Is there an hour or two when you can see each other? Can you make that quality time? Working out a plan for spending time together is important for both of you.

How *Not* to Communicate

Communication? Rare. I say, "Let's go talk about it."

It's like, "Wait a minute, I have to do this and that."

Finally when I have had it, I lose control. I get really upset.

Stephanie, 18/Kent, 20 (Sativa, 8 months)

There are lots of ways *not* to communicate with your partner. Always being busy with the kids or with projects in the garage reduces opportunities to talk with one's spouse. Leaving the TV on discourages talking. So does reading the paper during dinner.

One way to work on this problem is to plan special times you can talk together as already suggested for Arlene and Alfonso. Maybe you'll take a walk together or have a romantic dinner by candlelight. Some couples find they talk more freely when they're eating out. If you have children, plan some time with your partner *without* the kids.

It's the times we eat together that help our communication. I don't like eating by myself, and I hope Angela doesn't like eating alone either.

Juan, 18/Angela, 16 (Vaneza, 7 months)

Let the silent partner choose the time to talk. When s/he does, LISTEN! Then give your partner feedback on what you think you've heard. Show that you're willing to accept feelings and frustrations.

This doesn't mean you always have to agree. But if your partner finds you really do listen and you obviously care, s/he may find it easier to talk with you. You need to know what's going on inside your partner's mind and your partner needs to have some idea of what you're thinking.

Writing Notes May Help

Some people find a good communication starter is to write their feelings down, then share that with the other person. Sky, married at 17 to Delbert, 16, said:

> *When we couldn't talk, I'd write him letters. At first, I wasn't writing the letters to him, just about him and my feelings about the situation. Then one time he found one and said, "What's this?"*
>
> *I said, "No, you can't read that."*
>
> *He said, "Why not?"*
>
> *I finally let him read it. He got kind of teary-eyed about it, and I think he understood my feelings better than he ever had before.*

Sometimes expressing one's feelings in writing makes those feelings somehow more real to the person reading about them. And some people can express their feelings better through writing than by talking.

> *That was a bad scene last summer. Everything had been building up for several months, and I let go. I blew, telling Lloyd everything I didn't like about our lives. He acted like he didn't even care. I went over to my girlfriend's house for two days.*
>
> *When I came home, Lloyd was here with a long*

letter saying he was sorry for the way he acted and he would try to do better. He said he didn't know why he did the things he did, but he would have to work it out somehow. That helped a lot.

Lloyd can write his feelings down on paper much easier than he can tell me. There are things on paper that you wouldn't think came out of Lloyd.

Jeananne, 17/Lloyd, 18

Sometimes one person tends to dominate the conversation, or changes the subject if it's an uncomfortable topic. Conya says she has this problem, and that writing notes sometimes works better than trying to talk with her partner:

If I tell Ryan something and it hurts him, he tries to turn it around and say something that hurts me. Sometimes when I talk with him, it's hard because he'll interrupt me. He'll bring something else up, and I can't finish what I was going to say.

So sometimes it's easier to write it down. Sometimes I leave a note there when I go to school so when Ryan wakes up, it's there. Most of the time, I give it to him.

He's more calm if I write a note than if I tell him to his face.

Conya, 19/Ryan, 21 (Liana, 11 months)

Marriage Encounter is a nation-wide program for married couples that focuses on written communication between partners as a means to enriching the relationship. Usually it's an organized weekend sponsored by a religious group. Several denominations sponsor Marriage Encounter weekends. If you're interested, call 1/800/795-LOVE for information. If you're engaged but not yet married or living together, you might be interested in attending Engaged Encounter. Call 303/753-9407.

Different Family Scripts

Most disagreements have no absolute right and wrong.
You'll see an incident differently than your partner sees it.
Often what seems to be a big problem can be understood by
looking at the life scripts each of you brought into your
relationship.

---

*Your partner may have grown up in a family
where people didn't talk much.*

In her family, perhaps dad did the laundry while mom
cooked. In his family, mom did both, but she didn't have
an outside job. Each partner may feel strongly that there is
only one "right" way to run a home—and often that is
based on the way the individual grew up.

How you communicate, too, is likely to be much like
your parents' methods. You and your partner may very
well be scripted into communicating in quite different
ways. If this is true, you'll need to work hard at learning
to understand each other.

You may do most of your communicating with words.
To you, words may be all-important. You can express your
feelings and your frustrations. You're willing to talk about
whatever is on your mind. Verbal communication is no
problem for you.

Your partner may have grown up in a family where
people didn't talk much. They didn't express their feelings
through words. If each of you is tolerant and understanding
of the other's ways, the situation will probably improve as
it did for Davina, 19, and Johnny Angel, 19. Davina said:

*We have real good communication now. If either of
us needs to talk about something, the other one can
kind of sense it. Then we talk.*

In the beginning, I was always the one to express

*myself, and he would hold back. I would tell him it
would be better, that we might last a little longer, if
he would talk to me. Little by little he started to talk
more, and to realize that it works better. Now he
doesn't hold back. I think maybe just letting him know
he should open up a little helped.*

*We get along well, I think because of the communi-
cation. We understand each other. We've been together four years, and we know one another very
well, so it's real easy to pick up on something.*

Communication is when something is going on inside
you and you give that to the other person. Expressing your
own feelings and learning to listen to the other person are
necessary in order for good communication to take place.
Good communication is a basic part of a good relationship
as Johnny Angel illustrates:

*We communicate very well. We pretty much can
say whatever we're feeling to each other. When I'm
feeling down, I let her know, or if I'm very tired, or
I'm feeling hurt, or I'm feeling worried, I tell Davina.
She will pat me on the back, and I'll do that for her.
Maybe that's why our relationship keeps getting
better.*

Johnny Angel and Davina have a good thing going. If
you and your partner sometimes have trouble communicating with each other, plan special times regularly when you
can each give the other full attention as you talk together.
Your communication and your relationship are likely
to improve.

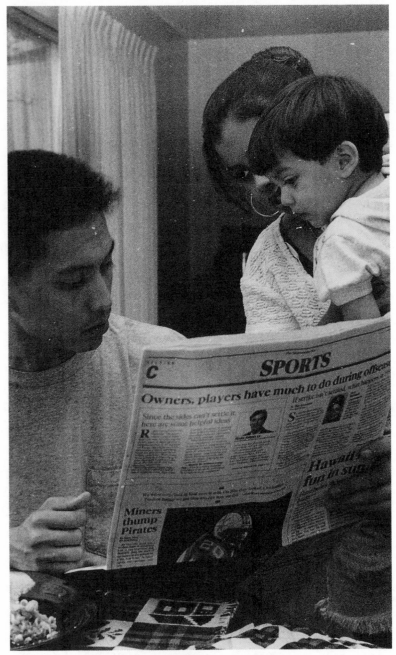

Refusing to talk doesn't solve anything.

CHAPTER 5

When Words Become Arguments

Before we got married, we'd go out, and we'd be so nice to each other. We wouldn't argue. Then after we got married two years ago, everything was still okay in the beginning. Then when Chianti was born, it was real hectic. We fight a lot now.

We fight about anything—washing clothes, who gets up with Chianti, whatever. We try to compromise like one day Judson will get up with her, and next day I'll get up. But it usually won't work that way because he'll get lazy or I'll get lazy.

We fight about who cleans up something. If he doesn't do it, I get mad. If I don't do it, he gets mad. We fight about our baby-sitter. When she couldn't come, somebody had to stay with Chianti. Judson said he couldn't miss work, so I'd usually stay home.

*Finally I said I just couldn't because I had to go to
school.*
Aracely, 18/Judson, 27 (Chianti, 18 months)

*We argue about going out. I like to go out with my
friends, and sometimes she won't let me. Sometimes I
won't let her go out with her friends. And each of us
would like the other to do more with the baby.*
Allan, 20/Denise, 17 (Lindsay, 8 months)

Communication with one's partner is important. Even a
couple who communicates well, however, will not always
agree. Many couples argue—or at least have serious, even
heated discussions. The ability to express differences
openly and frankly is important to your relationship.

Rules for Arguing

Arguments often are not fun. In the middle of a heated
discussion, people may say things they don't mean. Instead
of solving the problem under discussion, sometimes the
argument makes it worse. There are ways to argue, however, that can keep the conversation productive.

*An I-message is likely to lead
to a problem-solving conversation.*

When you drive your car, your bicycle or motorcycle,
you follow safe driving rules. Following rules when you
argue is also important.

- When you argue, attack the problem, not each other.
- Stay in the present. Learn to forget what happened
  yesterday when you're discussing today's problems.
- Don't accuse and run away.
- Try to avoid such words as "You always," "You
  never," or "Every time you . . ."

- Don't resort to petty name calling.
- Stay on the subject—and don't put down your partner's relatives!
- Express what you want instead of harping on what you don't want.
- When you're expressing your feelings, keep to the I-messages.

Instead of saying, "Where have you been all evening?" try "I was worried (or lonely or . . .) because you weren't here tonight." Instead of saying, "You're spending too much money," try "I'm terribly concerned because we can't pay our bills. I'd like to do something about it."

Chances are that your partner will respond cooperatively to your I-messages. Being put on the defensive is a waste of time. That's what you do when you accuse. An I-message is likely to lead to a problem-solving conversation.

> *When James and I lived together, we talked, but it wasn't good communication. There's bad communication and good communication, and ours was bad. When we would talk, we'd put each other down.*
>
> *Finally I learned to start with I-messages. "I feel angry." Before, I'd say, "Why didn't you take the trash out?" We could never just sit down and discuss. It would always end in an argument. Or he'd hit or throw something.*

Angelica, 18 (Jacari, 3 years)

Is It Worth a Fight?

A good question to ask yourself when you feel an argument brewing is, "Is this issue worth fighting over?"

> *You have to learn to separate what you're arguing about right then from your love and your life. You*

*can't let a stupid little thing ruin things. We used to
fight real bad. Then we realized it wasn't worth it.
Now when we fight, it's over something that matters.*

Josh, 19/Irene, 19

When you argue about something, try asking yourself
these questions:

- What do I want to gain out of this discussion?
- What does my spouse want?
- What will I have to do in order to satisfy my needs and
  my partner's needs in this area?

Hopefully, your partner is asking him/herself the same
questions.

Feedback: *Expressing in your own words
what you hear the other person say.*

If it is your issue, state your case clearly, then ask for
feedback. Listen to your partner's feedback. You'll learn
whether s/he really heard you or not. Then respond to the
feedback.

*Sometimes we stop and say, "Why are we fighting
over something stupid?" But it's getting harder as
our relationship develops. As we get closer together,
it's actually harder. It's like he wants to run everything as we get closer together. He wants to own
everything.*

Shannon, 17/Steve, 17 (Koary, 4 months)

Shannon could try this plan with Steve. She could say,
"I feel I'm not really a partner in our decisions. I don't
want to fight over this, but I need to help make this decision." She could then listen carefully to Steve's feedback.
If he doesn't really hear her, she might try to find another

way to express her feelings. If she can do this without becoming angry, Steve may finally listen. Together they may be able to work it out.

Don't Accuse and Run Away

He's always had a big temper, with yelling and screaming. He had a lot of frustrations growing up. He still wanted to be a kid, but now he's a daddy. It helped a lot when he learned to talk instead of screaming or just walking out.

I hated that when he'd walk out and come back hours later. He'd come back as if nothing had happened.

Meghan, 18/Justin, 21 (Jameka, 21/2 years)

Laying all your frustrations out on your partner, then walking away saying, "I don't want to talk about it anymore," isn't playing fair. You don't solve anything by saying your piece, then stopping the conversation.

Just as frustrating is the partner who hears you out, then refuses to respond. Again, "I don't want to talk about it" or, even worse, a cold silence solves nothing.

When Traci gets mad, she don't talk to me. When I do something wrong, she won't talk to me. She just blows it off. I try to talk to her and she gets mad, so I quit trying. Finally I forget it.

Wesley, 20/Traci, 16 (Elias, 20 months)

Once you and your partner have discussed your problem, however, and found a solution, then by all means drop it. Bringing up yesterday's argument is an emotional waste for both of you.

Several couples mentioned following the rule, "Don't go to sleep on your anger." It's important even if you've been fighting, always to kiss each other good-night.

*We went to dinner with Jeremy's great-aunt one
time. She told us that if we were having a disagree-
ment, we shouldn't go to bed without solving it. We've
done that, and it works.*

Marlene, 16/Jeremy, 19 (Amber Marie, 7 months)

Stick to the Subject

Many people bring in other issues. When an argument
starts, it's important to stick to the subject. Always
remember to attack the problem, not each other.

When you're arguing, realize that "You never" or "You
always" aren't allowed! "You never take out the trash,"
"You always nag me about that" are not helpful comments.
Is your goal to have a closer relationship with your mate
and to solve problems in the process? Then it's important
that you avoid putting your partner down with such
accusations.

Have you heard about the "ping-pong" method of communication?

She says, "You're no good."

He says, "You're no good, either."

She says . . . and on they go, passing insults back and
forth like a ping-pong ball.

It takes only one person to stop playing this game. If he
calls you names, and you say, "I really feel hurt right now,"
there's no way for him to hit back. Try it the next time you
and your partner start a verbal ping-pong game.

Have you heard the term "gunny sacking"? This refers
to storing up lots of complaints—putting them in the
"gunny sack"—then dumping them on the other person all
at once.

It's a bad scene anytime, and you can be sure gunny-
sacking won't help a relationship. When you're arguing,
stick to the subject rather than bringing in a bunch of other
complaints.

Dealing with Anger

We yell and scream at each other. Screaming gets the initial thing off your chest. Then we go back and talk about it. "Why do you go out all the time?" "Why don't you take me out?" "Why don't you do the dishes?"

He doesn't say much of anything—he keeps most of it inside, which is bad. I don't know what's eating him until he talks.

Elise, 18/Hector, 20

Nearly two out of three of the young couples in the Marriage Expectations Survey say they usually solve their arguments by talking. One out of four young men and one out of three young women, however, included yelling as a problem-solving technique. About the same number of each sex said they quit talking when an argument starts.

No matter how much you try to stick to the subject and how intently you listen to your partner, sometimes you're going to be angry. Expressing anger is okay. People who constantly bury their anger tend to have stomachaches.

We try to talk things out but sometimes we just have to walk away from each other for awhile and calm down. Most of the time we can talk. Most of the time we can share our feelings. It takes awhile, but usually we get them out.

Shanna, 18/Randy, 21 (Larissa, 15 months; Myndee, 1 week)

When you're furious, you may say things you don't even mean, things hurtful to your partner. An approach that may help is sharing your feelings early in the discussion.

Say "I'm getting angry." But don't accuse—don't say, "You're making me angry."

Sometimes it helps to say, "Let's stop this discussion for now. I'm saying things I don't mean, and I don't want this

to happen. Let's talk about it tomorrow." This is a big order
if you're really angry. Or you might try Dale's approach:

> *Dale's dad was into hitting his mother. I think he
> tries to be calm when we argue because he knows he
> doesn't want that. But lots of times he'll get mad—
> and then he'll sit down and he'll actually count, "1-2-
> 3-4." Then he'll say, "Well, I'm ready to talk."*
>
> *Sometimes it makes me laugh, and that stops the
> whole argument.*
>
> Betty, 20/Dale, 20 (Chrissie, 3)

Randy doesn't like to argue in front of his child. He feels
he and Shanna are better able to discuss problems now than
during their early months together:

> *If we get really mad, I try to take a second to calm
> down. Once in awhile we yell back and forth, but then
> Larissa cries. That makes us calm down for a couple
> of hours, and then we talk about it.*
>
> *When we argue now, we seem lots more able to
> talk it out than we could before. We've changed a lot.
> We act more mature. We used to get mad and stomp
> around, yell at each other. Sometimes it still happens,
> but not for long. I can't be physically violent to her
> because watching my dad do that made me sick.*
>
> Randy

Children get upset when they hear their parents arguing.
If the arguing becomes verbal abuse or physical violence,
the child will feel devastated. Make sure your child doesn't
have to endure that pain.

Both Dale and Randy were outspoken about guarding
against physical violence *because* their fathers had abused
their mothers. The sad reality is that, statistically, a man is
more likely to hit his partner if his father abused his

mother. Whatever you or your partner's growing-up situation, do *anything* to avoid becoming violent as you argue.

If you or your partner ever have trouble with your temper, you might talk about the possible need for a "time-out." This doesn't mean either of you packs everything and slams out of the house. A "time-out" is preplanned. If you get into something you can't handle, who will leave?

If you have a child, someone has to stay with her. If either of you has been drinking, you don't want that person to drive. The idea is that you have a plan if needed. Then if you're the one who stays home and your partner leaves, you won't think, "My mate has left forever." You're simply following the plan you made together.

> *When we're upset, we try to talk about it. When there's a real big argument, he goes home and I stay here until we both cool down. Then we talk about it.*
> Lupe, 18/Darren, 17 (Beau, 3 months)

Whenever there is any fear of violence, there certainly needs to be a time-out . . . a place for one of you to go until things cool down.

If the Woman Hits the Man

Chapter 10 is devoted to the tragic problem of partner abuse, and stresses how important it is for a woman to leave an abusive partner.

But what about women hitting men?

> *Women think they can hit a man and hit him and hit him. Sometimes Mitzuko is just playing, I know, but she's hitting me hard, and it hurts.*
> Maurice, 21/Mitzuko, 16 (Lana, 14 months)

As discussed in chapter 10, most women are far less likely to physically harm a man by hitting him. If she's smaller than he is, she probably can't hurt him as much as he can hurt her.

No one deserves to be abused, male or female.
Hitting is wrong.

Does this mean it's okay for a woman to hit a man? Of course not. No one deserves to be abused, male or female. Hitting is wrong. Hurting the other person is *not* the way to build a loving, caring relationship.

Partner abuse is very, very tragic. The hitting should never start. This rule applies to both men and women. If, however, a woman hits a man, whether or not she hurts him, her act does not give him an excuse to hit her. Jeremiah understands this:

> *We had a couple of fights, not brutal fights. No, no,*
> *it's not still going on. A little before we got married it*
> *happened.*
> *What stopped it? I'm not the kind of guy that likes*
> *to hit a woman anyway. It was really her attacking*
> *me, and it was me fighting her off.*
> *I stopped it. If I see a fight coming on, I leave. The*
> *guy should always leave, no matter what. I've heard*
> *girls say they can't hurt a guy by hitting him, but*
> *that's wrong.*
>
> Jeremiah, 21/Candi, 20 (Jakela, 2; Kamika, 1)

Jeremiah has mastered a very basic truth. Partners are not for hitting.

Wish List Approach

Some couples approach problem-solving with wish lists. Each makes out an "I wish you would" list. Make each "I wish" something specific that could possibly be changed. Then compare lists and negotiate.

He might write:

1. I wish you'd quit complaining when I go out with my friends.
2. I wish you wouldn't visit your mother so often.
3. I wish you'd keep the house cleaner.

Her list might be:

1. I wish you'd put the baby to bed at night.
2. I wish you'd pick up after yourself.
3. I wish you'd stay home more.

Negotiating means each gives a little. Can they each offer to satisfy one of the other's wishes? Perhaps she'll keep the house cleaner if he'll pick up after himself. If he bathes the baby, she'll have time to clean up the kitchen. Or she might say she'll quit nagging him about going out with his friends if he'll bathe the baby before he leaves.

Wish lists are a good place to start when you're looking for compromise solutions to your problems. Remember that it's important to stay on the subject when you're discussing these lists. Be positive, and don't turn it into another session in which each of you criticizes the other unmercifully.

When you're discussing your list, stick to expressing your own feelings. Don't evaluate or criticize your partner. That almost never solves anything. It's important that you take responsibility for solving your own problems.

Perhaps your partner seems always to be bad-tempered and inconsiderate. If so, you might try being positive every time you possibly can for at least three weeks. You may find your partner's disposition improves.

Who's in Control?

Our biggest problem is my attitude—and his attitude. We both want to control. We both want to tell each other what to do, who to talk to, where to go.

*I try to change, but it doesn't work. I wish we
hadn't started living together. I wish I'd waited.*
Dawn, 18/Mario, 18 (Tatiana, 1 month)

When you love your child, you are, to some extent
(depending on your child's age and maturity) in charge of
that child. When you're married and/or living with a partner, however, your relationship will be stronger if neither
of you takes on either the child role or the parent role.

*I want to be in control, but I pay attention to her
opinion. We don't need to do everything I say. If she
has an opinion and I agree on it, that's fine. It's a
different story when I disagree. I want her to enjoy
herself, and I care about her opinions.*

*But there are times . . . When I expect something
from Angela—like I ask her to stay home and she
refuses. She makes me talk and explain myself, tell
her why I don't want her to go out. Then she still tells
me "No." That really frustrates me. It's like explain-
ing my whole situation for nothing.*
Juan, 18/Angela, 16 (Vaneza, 7 months)

Juan doesn't realize how much like a father he sounds.
"I want to be in control, but I pay attention to her opinion"
is a good rule for parents of pre-schoolers to follow. It's *not*
enough for a true partnership.

Perhaps at first Angela more or less accepted Juan's
take-charge attitude. As she matures, she realizes she must
be an equal partner, and that she and Juan need to work
through this "Who's in charge?" question.

Neither of you is "in charge." Or rather, you're *both* in
charge—together. You each want to make the best decisions for both of you, and at the same time, you need to
respect your partner's decisions. Compromise is an
important part of a good relationship.

In a true partnership, each expresses wants and needs to the other. Each also listens to the other, and values the partner's opinions. Neither is "in control"; rather, both are in control of their life together. It's a hard-to-reach goal, but absolutely worth the effort to achieve it.

Communication is especially important if one or both of you has a strong urge to control the other one. Meghan and Justin are making progress toward becoming true partners:

> *Just recently we've been able to talk through problems—he's starting to grow up. He's learned he gets a lot further when he talks with me rather than just telling me what to do. I like talking to him. I think his counseling is helping.*
>
> Meghan

There is some conflict in every marriage. No two people agree on everything all the time. How you and your partner deal with that conflict can make or break your relationship.

You probably won't ever get over arguing with your partner, at least occasionally, as long as you stay together. Talk about it, compromise, never hit or insult each other, and your relationship, your love and caring can continue to grow.

Plan now how you'll keep romance alive in your relationship.

CHAPTER 6

Keeping
Romance Alive

*We try to do something together at least once a
week. We also each try to get out by ourselves once a
week. You need your own space.*

*It's good just to get out, go shopping, or walk
around. My mom will keep the baby for an hour
occasionally. That's when we try not to keep our
minds on the baby because that's when we stress out.*

*I work at least 40 hours each week and go to
school. Jarrod is with the baby when I'm at work, and
in the morning, when he's at work, I take the baby
to school.*

*It's real hard and stressful. That's why we try to
get out on the weekend. I can't take staying in the
house and letting it all build up.*

Anita, 18/Jarrod, 25 (Jarrod, Jr., 4 months)

Being "in love" is not enough to keep a relationship going well. Sooner or later the real world intrudes. The money problems and the arguments start. The baby comes, and, in addition to bringing you joy, keeps you both too busy to pay much attention to each other. People change, and if your relationship doesn't change, too, it won't work very well.

> *When James and I were living together, we didn't have fun. There was always something to do, something to take care of. The only thing that could have made it better was if we both had worked at it real hard. We were too young for all the responsibility.*
>
> Angelica, 18 (Jacari, 3 years)

So what's a couple to do? Enjoy each other if it's easy, and break up if it's not? Some people would say "Yes." Most likely you would rather have a lasting relationship, perhaps a forever one, or you wouldn't be reading this book. What can you do to achieve this goal?

Finding Time for Each Other

> *What's my biggest problem? When Allan closes up where he works, he doesn't get home until 3 a.m. Then he sleeps all day and I don't get to see him. I understand, but I'd like to see him. We hardly have any time to talk.*
>
> Denise, 17/Allan, 20 (Lindsay, 8 months)

Many teenage couples are terribly busy with jobs, school, and, for some, a child. Finding time for each other is difficult.

> *I'm working and Nathan has two jobs, plus we're both in school. That's a handful. We get tired, and we have to take time for ourselves. We put the baby to*

bed and sit down and relax. Sometimes we get a
babysitter for a couple of hours and go out shopping
or something.

Our relationship has gotten stronger in the three
years we've been together. We both understand that
we need time alone. We can't be with the same person
24 hours a day, seven days a week. We each need
friends and time to be by ourselves.

Katelynn, 17/Nathan, 20 (Daron, 2½ years)

Katelynn and Nathan have figured out a couple of
important ingredients for a loving, long-lasting relationship. They make time to be together. They also realize
each needs friends and some time alone.

Evenings together can be
valuable relationship-building times.

Putting the baby to bed at a regular time each night, and
making that time a couple of hours before the parents'
bedtime, is wise for two reasons.

One big reason for putting baby to bed at a regular time
is to give you and your partner some time alone together.
That's important.

Second, babies do better with regular schedules. Even
the toddler who has had no regular bedtime can adapt to
such a schedule if his parents devote two or three weeks to
teaching him to adjust through a bedtime routine coupled
with the firm comment, "This is your bedtime." For some
children, used to falling asleep at odd hours, this change
may not be easy.

For help, see a good parenting book such as *Teens
Parenting: The Challenge of Toddlers* (1991: Morning
Glory Press) or Vicki Lanski's *Getting Your Child to Sleep
. . . and Back to Sleep* (1991: The Book Peddlers).

Your time together after your child is in bed—or your evenings together if you don't have a child—can be valuable relationship-building times. Many people spend most of their evenings watching TV. If you both like to watch TV, and you can agree on *what* you watch, this may be fine. However, watching TV makes conversation impossible. Perhaps you'll decide to have one evening (or more) when you don't turn the TV on. Or perhaps you'll spend time regularly talking over a leisurely dinner before the TV goes on.

Do You Eat Together?

Mealtime traditionally has been a time for families to talk together, to enjoy each other's company. However, some families seldom have a meal together:

> *Normally we each make stuff we want to eat. Mario and I usually don't eat together. Everybody just eats whenever they're hungry. That's how it was at my mother's, too. I don't know whether Mario's family ate together or not.*
>
> Dawn, 18/Mario, 18 (Tatiana, one month)

> *At home we never had an actual sit-down meal where everybody sat down at the table at once and ate. Here we try to wait until everybody gets home to eat. I think it's nice.*
>
> Tiffany, 18/Shaun, 19 (Keosha, 11 months)

Juan and Angela find mealtime is the time they talk:

> *Meals are an important part of our relationship. We like to talk a lot. It sort of paces everything. I believe in tradition a whole lot. The longer you eat, the better. If you aren't just sitting there shoveling it down, you can enjoy it, talk, relate.*

For some people, eating by candlelight is special.

If Angela makes pork chops, vegetables, and some rice, we take our time eating it. But if you whip up some burritos, and you sit there and take quick bites, you're through. You don't even need a plate with a burrito, but with pork chops, you need a plate. A meal is a pace-setter.

Juan, 18/Angela, 16 (Vaneza, 7 months)

Several of the young couples I interviewed spoke of occasional candlelight dinners at home. Eating by candlelight, for some people, makes a meal special. The couple eating together by candlelight may realize—again—that they are special, too.

Jeremiah and Candi shared several ideas for keeping a relationship special:

About once a week we have a candlelight dinner with the kids. We like it and so do they.

*We go to the park and other places as much as
we can.*

*We don't go out no more. There's no money to go
out. We go to her mother's house or to my mom's.*
Jeremiah, 21/ Candi, 20 (Jakela, 2; Kamika, 1)

*I try to give Jeremiah a lot of attention because
that makes him happy. I buy gowns that he likes to see
me in. Sometimes I candlelight our bedroom. Or we'll
take the kids to a parent's house and have the house
to ourselves.*

*I think we need to be alone sometimes when we
have too much pressure. I fix dinner, clean the house,
look the way he wants me to look. We don't have a lot
of time for ourselves now, but we'll have all the time
we need when they grow up.*

*Sometimes we'll just walk through the park by
ourselves. It was hard in the beginning, but it's
getting better.*

Candi

Doing things together is an important part of building a
relationship. Pitching in together on cleaning up the house
on Saturday morning or doing the gardening as a team can
be more fun than doing either task alone.

Bathing the baby is a good team project. Enjoying music
together, reading the paper, watching TV, all can be building blocks for a growing relationship. Perhaps most important is finding time alone together:

*Just being together. We like to spend time together.
We go bowling, but we like it better when we're
alone. It seems like there's always somebody here. I
think that's the funnest time we have, when we're
alone.*

Sandra, 18/Troy, 21 (Violet, 16 weeks)

How Much Togetherness?

In an ideal relationship, would the partners spend all their time together? Probably not. Usually it works best if each person has his or her independent interests in addition to enjoying the time they spend together.

> *I like to do things on my own, like go out with my friends or play softball. Jarrod likes to watch me play.*
> *We like to go to movies—He's really into movies. And we both like to work out, although we usually do that separately.*

> Anita

If you find you disagree often on what you want to do, a solution can be more difficult:

> *We often don't like the same thing, and sometimes it's a problem. I want to go to the movies and he won't. Or I want to go see my mom and he wants to look at car parts. He goes his way and I go mine. Sometimes I look at car parts with him for awhile. and then he joins me at the movies.*

> Shannon, 17/Steve, 17 (Koary, 4 months)

Compromise is the key here. If you like movies and your partner doesn't, you may choose to go to the theater alone. Or perhaps you and your partner will decide to see a movie this week, and next week you'll do something your mate likes to do.

Sometimes a person learns to enjoy something *because* the partner enjoys that activity:

> *We both like going to basketball games. At first, Angela didn't. Like when I first met her, if I'd say, "Hey, let's go to a basketball game," she'd think I was crazy. That has changed. She likes basketball now. She's even interested in my card trading.*

> Juan

Saying "I Love You"

Some people who are quite demonstrative with their affection during the courting stage become less so after they start living together. This bothers Carman a lot:

Living with Caesar was good in the beginning. I guess now he doesn't love me as much as he did before because he's not as nice now. You know at first, they're all sweet and nice, and then it all fades.

I talk to him about it, but he says I'm crazy. He says he loves me the same. He says he shouldn't have to tell me he loves me because I already know he

"It feels good to have someone who cares."

does. I tell him I love him, but he doesn't tell me as
often. I don't know what it is. I guess he just might be
tired of us being together.

Carman, 16/Caesar, 21 (Sergio, 2 years)

For some people, saying "I love you" simply isn't
important. Probably Caesar really does love Carman, but he
doesn't think it's necessary to tell her again. To her, the
words are important. Perhaps as their relationship develops,
Carman will feel more secure and not need the "I love you"
words so often. And Caesar may begin to understand that
saying those words really isn't so hard, and if it's that
important to Carman, he'll say them more often. Hopefully,
this difference in thinking won't damage this couple's
relationship.

Saying "I love you" is one way of showing one's love.
Other ways can be just as valuable.

We always tell each other we love each other, and
that means a lot to both of us. And when we go
places, like the beach last week, we get pictures.

I love spending time with Mitzuko and the baby.
Plus Mitzuko takes care of me, man. I've never had
nobody worry about me before, and it feels good to
have someone who cares.

No one before ever asked me if I've eaten any-
thing, not even my mom. Mitzuko takes care of me
when I'm sick—she looks out for me. We really love
each other.

Maurice, 21/Mitzuko, 16 (Lana, 14 months)

Caring for each other sounds like a simple idea, but what
an important concept! Maurice's "It feels good to have
someone who cares" illustrates the love he and Mitzuko
feel for each other.

Selia and Enrique

Selia and Enrique are both 19. Their son, Riquie, is
almost a year old, and Selia is pregnant. They talked at
length about their marriage and shared many ideas on
keeping romance alive, techniques they have developed
in their relationship:

Selia: *My mom and aunt both tell us that once a
month we can leave the baby with one of them and
have a night by ourselves. My mom says we need to
spend time by ourselves.*

Saturday night is ours.
We turn the phone off, and that's our time.

---

*I think our relationship is great. It's basically
because we're more friends than husband and wife.
Me and Enrique are best friends. My girlfriends and
my mom told me before we were married that once we
got married we wouldn't have any fun any more. But
we have fun.*

*Sometimes Enrique brings home surprise flowers.
Or he'll come up the stairs and say, "Selia, you're so
pretty." I think you keep courting. If you stop
courting, you stop loving.*

*Saturday night is ours. We turn the phone off, and
that's ours. You have to do that. To keep a relationship alive, there has to be some time for just you
and him.*

Enrique: *Every problem that we have, we're still
growing. We're going through changes. I'm still
learning how to be a strong man for my family. As
Selia said, courting is what keeps the relationship
alive. Some relationships turn into water, and you
have to add that wine to it.*

Selia: *You have to do some things the other person likes and you don't. Like he wants to go camping and I really don't care about dirt in my food and I have hay fever. I keep saying "No." But if he comes home Friday and says, "Let's go," I'll go out and buy some bug spray and go.*

Enrique: *It's the little things that count. Every day I'm at work she can expect me to call her at a specific time and tell her I love her. I tell her—and this is true—that if I don't make this call, my day won't go right.*

Selia: *And he never leaves in the morning without telling me "Bye," even if I'm still asleep. One day he didn't do that because he was late. So the next time he was late, he ran all the way back up the stairs to tell me good-bye.*

Enrique: *Sometimes I want some time for myself. I think about things that will help our relationship, keep the wine flowing. First of all, communication needs to be stressed a lot. When we talk, sometimes I ask Selia how she feels about our relationship. What could be added to it? What would she like to do? Where would she like to go? This gives me data, information I can work on.*

One time we were about to have sex, and I asked her to go out on the porch in the rain. It's crazy, it increases the drive. So we had sex on the porch.

It can be things like just going outside and walking around and laughing and joking, being kids again.

Selia: *We create moments that when we sit down three or four months later, we can look back and laugh. Just last night we were sitting at the kitchen table talking about how we first met. We talk about stuff that happened last year, and now it makes us laugh.*

Enrique: *When we first got married, there wasn't much joy. I guess it was me. This father thing had me upset. Selia said I was like a 40-year-old man in a teen's body. I had to pay the bills, and we didn't have time for play. There wasn't much laughter. I had this stern look on my face.*

Selia: *He even makes the baby laugh now. Even during depressing times, Enrique will say something funny. Bills can get to you, and I get depressed quickly. One time we didn't have enough money to pay the phone and the gas bill. That got me mad and depressed, plus I ran out of Pampers. Running out of Pampers was terrible. I thought I was a bad mother.*

Enrique was telling me we'd get them. Then he comes in and says something silly, and my whole day changes.

We made a vow to each other
not to ever go to sleep mad at each other,
and never to sleep in separate rooms.

When he says I should give him his space, I question him. That's because I know he has a lot of pressure, and in the vows, it's for better or worse. I don't want him to face all this himself. When he says he wants to think, I immediately wonder, "Is there a bill we can't pay? Am I getting on his nerves?" He has a tendency to hold things in. I don't think he gets mad when I question. In fact, I think he kind of likes the fact that I'm concerned.

Enrique: *We made a vow to each other not to ever go to sleep mad at each other, and never to sleep in separate rooms. To be honest, we argue, but we've never been mad at each other for longer than a day.*

Selia: *I've given him the silent treatment for up to three hours—and, actually, it's not always silent.*

Being married and having a baby. . . Enrique is my baby, too. Not in the sense that he's babyish or anything. I say that because all day I tend to Riquie, and when Enrique comes home, sometimes I don't have time to say, "How was your day today?" Sometimes we can't even sit down for ten minutes together because we're both so tired.

That's why I say Saturday night is our night. I put Riquie to bed and I baby my husband. We baby each other.

If you and your partner, like Selia and Enrique, give each other extra attention, love, and caring, your relationship is likely to flourish. If you both continue to cherish each other, chances are good that your relationship will grow into the loving and caring forever experience you both want.

*A couple's sexual relationship depends to a great extent
on their total relationship.*

CHAPTER **7**

Sex Begins
in the Kitchen

We try not to base our relationship on sex or to let it interfere with our relationship. Sometimes I see couples getting carried away with that—they don't seem to have much else in their relationship. I don't think sex is a real important part. Communication is the best part.

Sue, 17/Rick, 20 (Jonathan, 7 months)

Sex Begins in the Kitchen is the title of a book by Dr. Kevin Leman (1992: Dell). Contrary to what you may be thinking, Dr. Leman does not suggest you and your spouse should make love regularly on the kitchen floor. Instead, he writes about the importance of your total relationship (including the time you spend together in the kitchen) and of its effect on the sexual part of your lives.

Effect of Total Relationship

How you and your spouse react to each other in bed is closely tied to how you act with each other the rest of the time. What you do together in the kitchen—and wherever you go—affects your sexual relationship.

*Our sexuality is part of us
in the same way our minds and our emotions
are part of us.*

Consider the amount of time you actually spend in preparation for and having sexual intercourse. If you're a highly sexed couple, this may be several hours each week. But even if it's an hour each day, that leaves 161 hours weekly for other activities. And most people spend much less than seven hours per week "having" sex.

How a couple treats each other during those 161-plus hours greatly influences their love-making. If she nags him every day about their terrible apartment and the fact that he makes very little money, he won't feel as loving as he might otherwise. If he puts her down constantly or if he's "out with the boys" several nights a week, she may not be thrilled about having sex with him.

Often, couples with sexual problems find, if they work at solving other problems in their lives, their sex life will also improve. Our sexuality is not a separate thing existing only in our genitals. It's part of us in the same way our minds and our emotions are part of us.

Communication is a vital part of any good relationship. That communication is important in developing a good sexual relationship. First, find out what you and your partner already know about the sexuality of men and women.

You may want to choose a good book on the subject, and learn or refresh your knowledge together. One excellent choice is *The New Teenage Body Book, Revised Edition* by Kathy McCoy and Charles Wibbelsman (1992: Putnam Publishing).

How Important Is Sex?

Nearly 70 percent of the young men and 60 percent of the young women in the Marriage Expectations Survey thought each spouse should be a good sex partner. Another quarter thought this was somewhat important. (These respondents were not yet married or living with a partner.)

In the survey of living-together couples, only one-quarter of the young men and even fewer of the young women said sex was "absolutely" an important part of their relationship. One-third of the males and females responded that it is somewhat important. The rest (almost half) said either "It doesn't matter," or sex is "not especially" or "absolutely not" an important part of their relationship.

In other words, teens living with a partner are much more likely to play down the importance of sex in their relationship than are teens not yet married or living with a partner.

> *You don't need sex to make a relationship go good. Sex is not the most important thing in a relationship. Really, you should be able to have a relationship without sex. Having sex changes your relationship a lot. Sometimes the guy thinks that's all a relationship is based on, and his partner will end up getting hurt.*
>
> Elaine, 19/Antonio, 17 (Kianna, 13 months; Sarah, 2 months)

Some, like Celina, don't think sex helps a relationship.

> *I enjoy sex, but I'm not the kind of person who wants it all the time. I think the more you have sex, the less close you are.*
>
> *When we started having sex, it changed our relationship. He didn't treat me the same as when we first*

*met. He didn't pay that much attention to me after
that. It wasn't the same. And when I was pregnant, I
didn't want sex. He'd want it, but I didn't.*

Celina, 17/Scott, 20 (Melanie, 6 weeks)

How Often?

People vary a great deal in how much or how often they
want to have intercourse. If both consider sex a very important part of their lives and want to "do it" twice a day, that's
fine. If neither thinks sex is all that important, and they
don't get around to having intercourse very often, that's
okay, too.

*My mom tells me, "It's real weird how you guys
never do nothing." After we got married and were
living by ourselves, we used to do stuff together, like
in bed.*

*A friend said the other day that she never sees us
kiss, and we don't. It takes about a month before we
do something in bed now.*

*Some people, they have to have it, and some people
really don't care. Like me and him, it don't really bug
us. It's only natural for a guy to want it once in
awhile, but it's not an everyday thing—just once
in awhile.*

Estella, 18/Joel, 20

Estella and Joel apparently have a satisfactory relationship. I do wonder about the meaning of "When we were
living by ourselves . . ." The lack of privacy since they
moved back with Estella's mother apparently has changed
their sex life.

The reassuring thing is that they seem to agree on this
important topic. Problems are more likely to occur if one
person wants to make love every night while the other one
is usually "too tired."

When You Don't Agree

Our relationship changed after we started having sex. It was more an emotional attachment.

For girls, you feel more for the guy, and you feel like any time he wants to, you have to. It's more of a pressure, something you worry about. You worry about getting pregnant. You worry about diseases. Our pregnancy was not planned. We used condoms, and I got pregnant anyway.

Actually, I think it would be best to wait until you're married because the emotional attachment, especially to your first, it's unbelievable. You want to feel that way for the person you're married to be-cause it's expected, and you know he won't leave the next day, and he didn't just use you.

Brenda, 17/Santos, 18 (Lydia, 4 months)

If you're feeling guilty about this relationship, that it isn't right to be having sex at this time, this undoubtedly influences your feelings. There are good reasons why many people think sex is okay only within marriage.

Apparently some teenage women don't like sex much. Often I have heard someone say it's something you "do" for men. Sometimes a discussion of sex turns into a discussion of how to get out of sex.

Sometimes he asks for too much sex. He likes to watch sex on TV, and that grosses me out. It makes him sexy, and it turns me off.

He practically asks every day. To me, sex is no excitement, it's just something that happens. I don't really enjoy it. So I say no most of the time. He gets mad, and then he sits back for awhile, or sometimes he convinces me.

Trina, 16/Victor, 16 (Felipe, 3 months)

If either you or your partner grew up thinking sex is ugly and disgusting, you may find it harder to have a satisfactory sexual relationship. If one partner feels relaxed and good about sexual activities, that partner may be able to help the other become more comfortable with the subject.

Talking about these things might add to Trina and Victor's understanding of each other's sexual needs and desires, or lack of those desires. That understanding might help them develop a more satisfying sexual relationship for each of them.

It is super important to remember that a good sex relationship usually takes time to develop. Learning to know each other, being able to talk about all parts of their partnership including the sexual part, and having plenty of time to experience each other can add up to a satisfying relationship. This doesn't happen overnight. *Good sex takes time.*

Talk and Compromise Are Essential

If you have an argument, sex is not the answer to that argument. Sex is not always the way of courting. You have to have communication.

Right after our baby was born, I wanted to do it, but I didn't want him to insert. I think the key is in that man constantly communicating with her. When Enrique started telling me how soft I was, how much he missed me, right after our baby was born, how pretty I was, I got horny. Words are very powerful.

Sometimes when she's pregnant, she's not ready for sex. I was sick all the time, and he really had to work with me. He'd come to bed and say, "You don't feel well," and he'd be rubbing my stomach the whole time. He'd say, "I just want to hold you and lie against you all night," and I'd turn over and be interested.

> *Just don't forget to talk about sex. My pastor told*
> *us the worst place to talk about sex is in the bedroom.*
> *Bring it up while you're watching TV, make it kind of*
> *fun. Don't make it to hurt feelings.*
>
> Selia, 19/Enrique, 19 (Riquie, 11 months)

If you disagree in other areas of your relationship, talk and compromise are important. Talk and compromise are just as important in disagreements over sex. However, there are added complications with sex. It's hard for most people to accept a turn-down from a partner in the bedroom.

Sex should not be a "should," something
one does because one is expected to.

If one's mate doesn't want eggs for breakfast, it's usually no big deal. But if that same mate, when approached for sex, says, "No, I'm not in the mood," the other person is likely to feel rejected. Somehow in our society we have this myth of both men and women being constantly ready for sex. If you don't believe it, watch the TV soap operas.

On the other hand, women, especially, are learning that it is important not to fake an interest in sex just to please a man. Sex should *not* be a "should," something that one does because one is expected to. It's okay to say, "Not this time."

> *I think pregnancy makes you less interested in sex.*
> *When I tell him "No," he seems to get his feelings*
> *hurt real bad. He's starting to understand, but not*
> *that much, that you go through changes in a preg-*
> *nancy, a lot of changes. I just don't feel like being*
> *bothered with it.*
>
> *He says I'm not romantic with him any longer. It*

went through my mind once, "What if he goes and
finds somebody else?" But he's not like that.
   It can also hurt the girl because she thinks she has
to be sexually active. It's very hard.

Janita, 16/Elijah, 19

It's important not to make your partner feel rejected.
It's also important not to force yourself to have sex if you
don't want to.

How do you do this? How do you help him feel you still
love him even as you say "No" to sex? Touching, being
warm, recognizing his feelings help. You can appreciate the
feelings he's expressing, as in "I know how you feel, but
tonight . . ."

The answer lies in compromise and communication.
Both partners need to consider each other's feelings and
their own. If they do, they will be better able to work out
answers for their own situation. Janita continued:

Communication comes into this. You have to talk
to the guy. That's how I got Elijah comfortable with
the idea. You have to talk and talk, explain to him
how you feel, and that this pregnancy won't last
forever. He needs to talk to her and tell her how he
feels, too. That's where the communication comes in.

If you don't talk, that little minor problem could
cause your relationship to be on the rocks. He'll think
she's losing interest in him, and she'll think, is he
going to run out there and find someone else? You
really have to talk about it.

A lot of books skip over this, or say just a little
about it. In school we have the group meetings. I
thought I was the only one who felt this way, but I
found a lot of girls feel the same way. And a lot of
guys don't understand why we feel this way.

Loving is an important part of life.

See *Teenage Couples: Coping with Reality,* Chapter 8, for suggestions concerning sexual intercourse during pregnancy and after childbirth.

Conflict of Expectations

Part of the problem is the difference in sex drive between men and women. Men tend to have a high sex drive in their teens while women are likely to become much more interested in sex a few years later.

The way I see it, the guy wants it all the time and the girl doesn't. You need to talk about what you like and what you don't. If you don't, you're not going to enjoy it at all. And there's so much to do, you just want to go to sleep.

Dawn, 18/Mario, 18 (Tatiana, 1 month)

If one partner is usually the one most interested in sex (among teenagers, this more often is the male), placing more attention on the desires of the other is very important. If she isn't as interested in sex as he would like, they need to learn to communicate their feelings about what feels good to each one. Caressing, intimacy, touching, and kissing are important—more important than intercourse to some people.

---

*You need to talk to each other
about what brings pleasure to each of you.*

Men and women often have different expectations for each other. Sometimes this is because of lack of experience with themselves and their own sexuality and of the sexuality of the opposite sex. They don't have a good understanding of male and female arousal, of what turns people on.

Different people feel comfortable with different things, and you two need to work that out in your relationship. You need to talk to each other about what brings pleasure to each of you. It's important that neither of you exploit the other by doing something that makes the partner uncomfortable.

In the beginning, he wanted a lot of sex and I didn't want much. He knew my problems and my hang-ups. He got mad a couple of times, but he coped.

When I was pregnant, I liked sex a lot. Now I have the Depo-Provera (contraceptive) *three-month shot,*

*and when it's wearing off, I like sex more. When I
first get it, I don't like sex much.*

*When Jeremiah's in the mood and I'm not, I pick
an argument. He likes me to caress him a lot. He feels
it's something everybody should like, but I don't
really like that. So I explained to him the reasons, and
he understood.*

Candi, 20/Jeremiah, 21 (Jakela, 2; Kamika, 1)

The fear of pregnancy can keep a woman from enjoying sex. She and her partner need to select a reliable method of birth control and use it *every* time they have intercourse. If they do, she is likely to become more interested in sex.

"Whose Fault Is It?"

In sex as in anything else, it's easy to blame the other person.

"It's her fault if I don't achieve great heights of sexual pleasure."

"If he knew what he was doing, I'd like it."

Blaming someone else doesn't change anything. Talking together about what feels good to each of you might help. And remind each other that a good sexual relationship takes time.

Karina and Vincent, married more than a year ago, are able to talk about the sexual part of their relationship:

*We started off having sex every day up to about
two months ago. I think too much of a good thing
spoils it. So I decided to make it more special. It's not
just sex. It's love. I like to be talked to during, but he
doesn't.*

*We talk about it. I tell him he's very good. I'm not
embarrassed to say it. He satisfies me—more than
satisfies me. We both like to try new things. We talk*

about it before, like "How would you like this?" If
one of us says, "I don't like it," then we don't.

I went out and bought lingerie for him, because I
know guys are more into seeing than touching, while I
like to be touched. I think what you do is you try new
things. I like spontaneity. I don't like to plan it. It
doesn't have to be just at night—sometimes during
the day out of the blue.

Karina, 16/Vincent, 20 (Saulo, 7 months)

Sex Is Not a Competition

Slang for the sex act generally is not very positive.
Competition—"Did you score?" "I didn't even get to first
base"—is often stressed in the way we talk about sex. In a
competitive sport, somebody wins and somebody loses.

If sex is going to be satisfying to a couple, however, it
will not be at all like competitive sports. It will be a coop-
erative venture, a time when two people can be together
and enjoy each other with no thought of one being inferior
or superior to the other.

Sex played a big part in our relationship. That was
one of the strengths. It's not the controlling part of
our lives, but it's in everything.

There are other important parts of a relationship,
but sex does help. It's a time when you and your
partner become closer. If you have problems, talk
about it. It's in everything. Don't let it ruin your
relationship.

Meghan, 18/Justin, 21 (Jameka, 2 1/2 years)

Men and women are different in more than the fact that
one has a penis, the other, a vagina. Most men are turned
on faster than women. For most men, intercourse is the
most important thing. For many women, the hugging and
cuddling is at least as important as the sex act itself.

A good sexual relationship is a good talking relationship. It's important that a couple talk about their wants. Only in this way can they understand they aren't always going to have the same needs. Lots of times, if you have mutual respect and caring, you can compromise.

This book is not meant to be a sex manual. If you want specific help with sex problems, there are some good books available. If you think your problems are too big to solve yourselves, you may decide to see a therapist. Ask your doctor or call your local mental health clinic for recommendations.

And remember—Sex begins in the kitchen!

Jealousy can seriously damage a relationship.

CHAPTER 8

Building Trust— Not Jealousy

I get jealous, and he does, too. We have a lot of problems with that. I get jealous of his workers because of my past relationships with other people. I've never been able to trust anybody. I put that on Jarrod, blame him for things. He does the same with me because of his past relationships.

Yes, we have a jealousy problem. For both of us, it's a problem left over from other people. Our trust has been growing. We've been together almost two years, and gradually it's getting better and better. We're starting to trust each other, give each other more space, and get along better.

Anita, 18/Jarrod, 25 (Jarrod, Jr., 4 1/2 months)

Everyone gets jealous at times, to a point, but it can get out of hand. If every guy you talk to and say,

"Hi," he wants to know why—that's getting out of hand.

Katelynn, 17/Nathan, 20 (Daron, 2 1/2 years)

Jealousy isn't even listed in the index of most marriage books. But many teenagers (and older people) find that their jealous, possessive, and anxious feelings cause them and their partners a lot of misery. An amazing number of arguments start with jealousy.

Conquering jealousy
is a positive step in most relationships.

Anyone experiencing jealousy knows these feelings are real, no matter what their source. If jealousy occurs because one's partner is actually having an affair with someone else, denying those feelings may not be healthy. If you feel jealous every time your partner looks at or talks with a person of the opposite sex, however, perhaps you need to work toward more acceptance of and trust in your partner. Conquering this kind of jealousy is a positive step in most relationships.

Marriage Survey Indicates Jealousy

Slightly more than half the teens responding to the Marriage Expectations Survey said they would be jealous if their partner "looked at" someone of the opposite sex. About 40 percent said they would be jealous if the partner talked with a person of the opposite sex. Among the teen men, 23 percent would be jealous if she worked with males, while fewer (15 percent) of the women indicated the same jealousy.

Three in four of the males don't want their partner to go to a concert with another boy, and even more of the females (84 percent) would be jealous of a concert date with the opposite sex. About half of the men, but only one-fourth of the women, would be jealous if the partner had a close friend of the opposite sex.

Why do so many of us have these jealous feelings? If we think about it, even going to a concert with another friend may make sense. I may not enjoy the same type of music my partner does. Or I may not be able to go on that particular night. If he has a friend who happens to be female, why should I be threatened if she keeps him company?

While our heads may tell us it's okay, many of us wouldn't cope well with such a situation. Feelings don't always make sense. Jealous feelings *often* don't make sense. But if they are your feelings—or your partner's feelings—it may not be important whether or not they make sense. Feelings are feelings. They are there, and we need to deal with them.

Reasons for Jealousy

Sometimes we're more "needy" and our jealous feelings are more intense.

For some couples, jealousy is carried over from past relationships. If she used to be with a man she couldn't trust, she may have trouble trusting a new partner, even if that partner has given her no reason to feel this way. Or his jealous feelings may be left over from a former relationship that turned sour.

I'm very, very jealous. He's not, but I am. Every time he goes somewhere, or if he talks to this girl he's known for a long time, it makes me jealous. I've been through a lot of problems with guys, so it makes it hard to trust him. I start arguing with him. He tries to calm me down, tells me no, nothing happened.

Trina, 16/Victor, 16 (Felipe, 3 months)

Feelings change. Sometimes we're more "needy" and
our jealous feelings are more intense. For instance, a
woman who is pregnant may be bothered more with jealousy than she was earlier. Some women don't feel as
attractive during pregnancy. She may think she looks fat,
and she may need a lot of reassurance. If her partner can't
or won't give her that reassurance, she may feel very hurt
over some incident he considers completely unimportant.
Melodie, 16, explained her feelings:

> *It was real strange because when I first went with
> Brett, he had been going around with a lot of girls.
> There was always somebody hanging on to him. At
> first it didn't bother me—until I was pregnant. That's
> when it started.*
>
> *He'd look at girls, and I'd get extremely jealous. It
> got so bad, so stupid—he would look at the TV, and it
> was bad. He would look at "Baywatch," and that
> bothered me! He couldn't do anything with females as
> far as I was concerned. He never did understand how
> I felt.*

Lack of Self-Esteem

The biggest reason for jealousy is probably lack of
self-esteem, of feeling good about oneself. If you're
bothered by your partner talking with someone of the
opposite sex, is it because you think your mate may like
that person better than you? Do you perhaps wonder
what your love sees in you?

If a woman feels insecure or anxious, having her partner
look at another woman might remind her that she herself
isn't as desirable as she'd like to be. A man who doesn't
see himself as a healthy human being is more likely to be
bothered if his wife talks with another man. He may feel
she is simply confirming his opinion that he isn't

everything she wants. This might explain Ryan's feelings:

> *Ryan is jealous of my ex-boyfriend. Ryan is always*
> *getting mad about that, but I'm not even talking to*
> *Jake. I haven't seen him for I don't know how long,*
> *and Ryan still gets mad at me.*
>
> *Like when I come to school and do my hair or put*
> *my make-up on, he says, "Why do you get all dressed*
> *up? Are you seeing somebody?"*
>
> Conya, 19/Ryan, 21 (Liana, 11 months)

Ryan is likely to become more self-confident as his
and Conya's relationship develops. This happened with
Johnny Angel:

> *My wife is very, very beautiful, and I used to get*
> *quite jealous. But it's turned me to where I take it as a*
> *compliment when other men glance at her. We're very*
> *committed to each other, and I don't feel she would*
> *go anywhere, and I wouldn't either.*
>
> *A young man that's secure—and that means being*
> *with somebody you'd plan a future with, somebody*
> *you'd be with for a long time. I saw that in my wife,*
> *and she saw that in me, and I'm not jealous. I know*
> *where she is and who her mind is on. But if I were*
> *dating some girl for six months and I got her preg-*
> *nant, I wouldn't really know how she feels about me.*
>
> Johnny Angel, 19/Davina, 19 (Valizette, 11 days)

Johnny Angel makes a good point. Too often, a teenage
couple starts a baby before they know each other very well.
He's likely to think, "She's carrying my baby. She
shouldn't even glance at other men."

She may decide, "I'm pregnant because of him. He has
no business noticing other girls. I need him too much."

The couple who doesn't take time to build a strong

relationship before entering the I-need-you stage of pregnancy needs to work hard at growing together while feeling secure enough as individuals to trust each other.

Discussing the Jealousy

If you're bothered with jealous feelings, it's important to try to understand what you're jealous of. What is really bothering you? If it's something that's not too hurtful to your partner, talk openly about it.

Open up, say how you feel. It's hard to bring up the subject sometimes, but it's important to do so, as Arlene and Alfonso learned:

> *I don't do anything, but he thinks that every guy that's passing by is looking at me. I asked him once, "Are you jealous because you're afraid of losing me?" He hates to admit it, but that's the way he is.*
>
> *I might glance at a guy, but I don't do nothing. If I go out, he'll say, "Be careful . . ." I talk to him about that.*
>
> *I'm not jealous. When he goes out, girls will whistle, and I think it's kind of cute.*
>
> *I tell him, "I'm your wife. Why worry about these little guys in the street?"*
>
> *He'll say, "Well, I worry."*
>
> *I'll say, "I'm not going to go follow them."*
>
> Arlene, 14/Alfonso, 16 (Sylvia, 4 months)

When you're talking about jealousy, don't accuse the other person. You aren't trying to hurt your partner. Instead, you want to reflect your own feelings. "This is how I feel when I see this happen."

Enrique, 19, and Selia, 19, talked freely about their feelings. They feel some jealousy is all right, but that it can go too far:

Enrique: *I'm a jealous person. This may be child-ish, but I don't like it when my wife talks to other men. I don't even like it when she smiles at them. I don't make a fool of myself, but I ask her about it. It drives me crazy.*

Selia: *I feel the same way. I don't like it when he talks to old girlfriends. When he sees one of those little girls, I ask him to stop it. But it's not bad be-cause me and him talk about it. I tell him, "Look, I'm jealous, so don't do it." When you get married, that's part of it. Anybody that says they aren't jealous is lying. But it can go too far.*

I've known girls whose boyfriends wouldn't let them go to school with boys, they were so jealous. That can drive them away. Those guys are closing in too tight. People have got to breathe.

Enrique and Selia have been together almost two years. Time may ease their jealous feelings as they become more comfortable with each other and feel more secure within their relationship.

Jealousy and Possessiveness

Jealousy is closely related to possessiveness. Sometimes one partner seems always to want to be with the other. It's as if the partner is a possession, a possession not to be shared with others.

> *If your partner is very possessive and doesn't want you to do anything alone, you're likely to feel resentful.*

For example, he may like to go out with the boys or play basketball all evening. She may be very jealous of his outside relationships and want him home every night. If he stays home to please her, he may be miserable. If he ignores her wishes, she'll be miserable.

She may want to go shopping with her friends, spend more time with her family, or go to parties with her pre-marriage crowd. He thinks both should stay home. Again, whatever the solution, it may cause unhappiness—unless one or both is willing to change.

His belief system allows him to go out but he thinks she should stay at home.

If your partner is very possessive and doesn't want you to do anything alone, you're likely to feel resentful. Desiree, 17, and André, 18, are no longer together because of André's possessiveness:

> *André constantly kept a tab on what I was doing, who I was with—but he could do whatever he wanted. He was always possessive, but it got worse. After Keisha was born, he was so possessive with me that I always had to stay home and care for her.*
>
> *We broke up about two months ago, and at first it was real hard. He didn't want me dating anyone else, and there was a lot of fighting.*
>
> *Eventually it worked out, and he realizes now that our relationship is over.*
>
> Desiree, 17/André, 18 (Keisha, 4 months)

Several of the teen women I interviewed talked about partners who didn't want them to see their friends—although some of those same partners continued to spend lots of time with *their* friends. It's almost like a kind of culture clash. His belief system allows him to go out but she should stay at home. This is a problem for Shannon:

> *I don't have time for my friends any more. Steve*
> *doesn't really want me to go out with my friends*
> *although he goes out with his. I'm getting kind of mad*
> *because he won't let me go see mine. He says, "It's*
> *because you see them all the time."*
> *I'll say, "Why do you go out?"*
> *And he says, "That's different."*
>
> Shannon, 17/Steve, 17 (Koary, 4 months)

Why is it different? This might be the time to discuss the idea of a role switch. How would Steve feel if Shannon insisted on seeing her friends but refused to "let" him see his? If it's because Koary needs care, they need to discuss the advantages of shared parenting.

The more Steve is involved with Koary's care—including being home with him occasionally while Shannon sees her friends—the more both Koary and Steve will benefit.

Talk About Feelings

Are you with a man who expects you to stay home with the baby every night while he's out partying with his friends? "I feel. . ." and "How do you feel. . ." conversations may help. "I feel lonely here by myself night after night." "How do you feel about seeing so little of our son?" Then really listen to his answer.

Sharing feelings is possible
without totally agreeing
with each other's point of view.

Nagging him, telling him how wrong he is, probably would be no help at all. Being interested in his feelings could start a conversation which might lead to some real sharing of feelings. Sharing feelings is possible without totally agreeing with each other's point of view. This often leads to more understanding of the other person. From such understanding can come a change in attitude, or at least a compromise.

If he's been spending two or three nights per week with his friends, is he willing to cut down to one? Can you go out with him another night each week? Often you can take your child with you on visits with friends. Or you could set up baby-sitting trades with other young parents.

Of course the problem may be the opposite. You may be the man in the relationship, and you wonder why your partner wants to go out all the time. Do you think she spends too much time with her friends? With her family? Perhaps you wonder why she doesn't stay home more.

"Feelings" conversation is again a good place to start. "How do you feel about staying home?" You may find she is very lonely. Or she may dislike being home because she hates to do housework. What you thought was a refusal to be the kind of partner you wanted may instead be her way of coping with a situation she doesn't like.

How can you help? You can understand the pain of feeling lonely and discuss ways of improving the situation. If she can't stand keeping house, perhaps she needs to get a job. Then you and she can share the housework and the financial responsibilities. If she needs more education or job training, perhaps together you can work out a way for her to return to school.

The above examples may be due to possessiveness, to anxiety, or to jealousy. All three are closely related feelings. If either partner feels possessive, finding activities you can enjoy together may solve much of the problem. Gradually the possessive partner may realize it's best for each person to have interests of his/her own in addition to shared activities.

*"Feelings" conversation sometimes helps
a couple deal with their jealousy.*

If Jealousy Is Severe

*Kent doesn't even trust me to go to school. He gets
mad at me for wearing make-up to the doctor's.
Sometimes he gets very upset. One time I was wearing
a white shirt, and it was tight. He took a lipstick and
wrote all over it. He can get violent although he
doesn't hit me. He takes it out on material things.
Like he got mad at me and he ripped my shoes.*

*He wants to control me. He tells me what to wear.
He wants to control my life, and I don't like that.
He's so possessive that sometimes he won't let me go
outside by myself. I feel trapped.*

*Everyone says, "Why don't you leave him?" But
that's easier to say than to do. I've been with him for
a long time. I've tried so many times to leave him, and*

*then he'll come up to me and say, "Oh, let's make
up." I have left, but I come back. That's the problem.*

*He was so polite to me in the beginning. He's
changed a lot. He was so nice to me. I'm jealous, too,
but not to the point that I'm so possessive of him.
When he wants to go out, I let him. But if I go out, I
have to explain so much to him.*

*I'm going to get a job. At first he said, "No,"
because in his country women stay home and take
care of the baby. Now he realizes we need the money
and he says, "Well, okay." He's so afraid of me
getting a guy and leaving him.*

Stephanie, 18/Kent, 20 (Satira, 8 months)

Eugenie Wheeler, A.C.S.W., listened to Stephanie's
story and commented, "This sounds like a classic abuse
case because the violence appears to be escalating. I think
Stephanie and Kent's problems could get a lot worse if they
don't get some kind of counseling.

"It's very important," she continued, "that Stephanie go
to work. She should also look at her own behavior—not
that it's her fault, not at all, but could she do more to build
Kent's confidence in her and in their relationship? Perhaps
she could stress their cultural differences in a discussion
with him."

Jealousy is always a function of insecurity, according to
Ms. Wheeler. She feels a couple must establish a pattern of
trust. "How could Stephanie help Kent feel a greater sense
of security in the relationship?" she asked.

Ms. Wheeler concluded that Kent's actions appear to be
a red flag, a danger signal that may point to physical
violence.

For a discussion of partner abuse and how to avoid or
stop it, see chapter 10. Or read *Breaking Free from Partner
Abuse* by Mary Marecek (1993: Morning Glory Press).

Dropping Out Because of Jealousy

There are many reasons for the high rate of school dropout among pregnant adolescents and school-age parents. In addition to financial problems and lack of child care, a mate's jealousy may be a big factor in the decision to quit school.

Sometimes a young man doesn't want his partner even to attend school because she "might talk to boys." Each year, when I was teaching, several young women would tell me they were dropping out of high school because their husband or boyfriend didn't want them there because there were other boys around.

Some young women want absolutely no reference to the partner's ex-girlfriends:

> *When he looks like he's thinking, I'll say, "What are you thinking about, your ex-girlfriend?" He has his high school scrapbook with pictures of him and his ex-girlfriend. I tell him to rip it up, but he won't.*
>
> *She and I used to talk, but since she knew I was with him, she started giving me these looks. It bothers me a lot because sometimes I think he's thinking about her.*
>
> Celina, 17/Scott, 20 (Melanie, six weeks)

Celina needs to realize she can't read Scott's mind. She can't know what he's thinking about. Accusing him of thinking about his ex-girlfriend helps no one. Tearing up pictures in his high school scrapbook may seem to Scott like throwing away part of his life.

Perhaps Scott can help Celina deal with her feelings by reminding her frequently that he's with her now, not his ex-girlfriend.

Jillian used to feel jealous when her husband talked with an ex-girlfriend. Then she looked at her reality, and said:

*I've learned that he picked me, not her, and he
must like me better. That's what I tell myself when I
feel threatened. That's my resolution to the problem.*

If either partner is so jealous that s/he doesn't want the
partner interacting at all with the opposite sex, a solution
may be more difficult. The world is filled with both men
and women. Interacting with only one sex plus one's
partner would be a difficult task for most of us.

Double Standard Lives On

Sometimes if one partner is quite a bit older than the
other, the older partner may worry about losing the younger
one. Perhaps this is part of Adam's concern. Crystal
described their situation:

*Sometimes Adam goes overboard. "What did you
wear today? What button did you have buttoned on
your shirt?" He especially annoyed me when I was
pregnant. I think he does it less now because I'm
home more. When I leave the house, I'm usually
with him.*

*Sometimes I'm jealous, too, but he thinks that's
silly. He doesn't see that he has a double standard.
What he sees as me being too free with someone is
only being friendly if he does it.*

Crystal, 17/Adam, 28 (Breanna, 10 months)

The double standard lives on in many relationships. And
it usually causes problems. Does Adam want Crystal to tell
him how to dress? Or perhaps she already does? Communicating their concerns to each other may help.

In a good relationship, both partners need to remember
neither owns the other. Each is an individual person. As
their relationship grows, each needs to realize this other
person, this loved partner, is *not* a possession.

Maybe Adam would play an imaging game with Crystal. Perhaps if he can imagine he is Crystal, and his partner is telling him what to wear and what not to wear, he'll understand her feelings a little better.

When you criticize your partner, is it okay if your partner criticizes you in the same way? If not, think about it—and then try harder to treat your mate as you would like to be treated.

Coping with Infidelity

Sometimes jealousy is based on fact. Too often men and women leave a still-loving partner for someone else. Or one might have a short-term affair thinking it won't harm the primary relationship. How should this be handled?

If the straying partner leaves for the new love, the other person needs to cope as well as possible. See chapter 11 for suggestions on dealing with this situation.

The Six-Months-Rule can save a relationship.

But if the straying partner really doesn't want out of the relationship, what then?

Some people immediately separate and file for divorce. "I won't put up with that," they say indignantly.

The sad part of such a situation is that sometimes the new love grows old very quickly. Often, the grass is *not* greener on the other side of the fence. The original relationship might have a good chance of succeeding in spite of the supposed break.

The Six-Months-Rule can save a relationship. Each promises not to make a final break from the relationship until at least six months after a problem occurs. Six months in one's lifetime isn't very long. And sometimes the problem has gone away or been resolved by the end of that six-month period. If you love someone, breaking off that relationship too quickly may be a sad mistake.

Rebuilding a trusting, loving relationship after infidelity has occurred is difficult. If the injured partner constantly brings up the incident saying, "I know I can't trust you anymore—look at what you did to me," love will be hard to regain. To forgive and forget is never easy. If you want to restore a good relationship, however, forgiving and forgetting are necessary.

If you have destroyed your partner's trust in you, you'll need to work hard on rebuilding that trust. If you plan to be faithful from now on, clearly expressing your intentions and your feelings will help. Put extra effort into demonstrating your intentions.

Even more important, show your partner constantly how much you trust, respect, and care for him/her. Love can grow again if both partners are willing to work hard enough to reach this goal.

Trust Develops Over Time

Many teens have jealous feelings early in their relationship. Then, as time passes, they feel more secure:

> *Before, I didn't want her wearing little short skirts except around me. But now it's different. I'm over that stuff. That was way back when we first got together.*

Sam, 18/Myra, 17

Katelynn and Nathan are a good example of trust development:

> *In the beginning we were both jealous. "Why are you looking at him?" "Why are you talking to that girl?" We kept on getting mad at each other and*

arguing. Then we realized it was stupid and we weren't going to let jealousy ruin our relationship.

Now we both understand that guys and girls can be friends.

Katelynn

Trust the one you're with. If she didn't want to be with you, she wouldn't be there.

We had problems when we first started going out because I've seen so many people get hurt. It's hard to build the trust. I was suspicious because I've seen too much. But now I figure if she didn't want to be with me, if she didn't love me, she wouldn't be here. If I had anything to worry about, she wouldn't want to marry me.

Nathan

Katelynn and Nathan are a wise couple. Jealousy left unchecked can destroy a relationship. Together, a couple can grow beyond jealousy. Their relationship will be stronger as their trust in each other becomes stronger.

Trust is an important part of a good relationship. If you can trust each other, you'll be ahead. Both of you will be happier if you have a high trust level.

Alcohol or drug addiction can destroy a relationship.

CHAPTER 9

Alcohol and Drugs— Time for Recovery

Before I met Emery, he used to drink all the time. That's not the way I am, and he changed his life around. Now we hang around mostly with the same people. I just told him I didn't like it, and if he didn't change, I was going to find somebody else.

He changed slowly. I had my mom talk to him, too. He's been clean for a long time. He doesn't drink, he doesn't do drugs. He spends a lot of time with me, more than he does with his friends.

April, 18/Emery Dean, 19 (Patrick, 22 months)

While I was pregnant, Kenny was always taking off. I didn't want him to go out drinking and get into trouble. When he'd come home, he'd try to fight me, then the next day he wouldn't remember.

Still to this day he likes to drink, but he's been all right the past couple of months.

We never used to talk to each other, hardly ever discussed anything. Now we can talk things over without arguing and fighting. And we know it's not good for Damian to watch us fight.

Kenny is on probation, and he has to go to AA (Alcoholics Anonymous) meetings. They last about an hour, and when he comes home, he usually tells me about it. I think those meetings are helping.

Misty, 18/Kenny, 17 (Damian, 11 months)

In every relationship, problems are bound to occur. Sometimes those problems go beyond arguments and jealousy and build into major difficulties.

Alcoholism, drug addiction, and violence can ruin lives. In the process, an otherwise valued relationship may be destroyed.

"He Drinks Too Much"

Many teenagers drink alcohol occasionally or regularly. Too much alcohol can damage a relationship quickly. Elaine described Antonio's struggle to quit drinking:

He drinks a lot. He would take off on a Friday and I wouldn't see him until Sunday. I'd be home by myself with the kids, and that's real hard.

He's trying to stop, but it will take a while. We're always fighting and arguing about that. He's been going to AA every week. They showed some kind of film the other night, and he said it made him look at it from a totally different point of view. He wants to do this, quit drinking, and he has kind of straightened up these last three weeks. It's not as hard as it used to be. He was court-ordered to go to AA—on probation until this June.

He was drinking before we even met. He's 17 now. It's mainly friends, they come around and they don't have responsibilities, and it's "Come on, Tony, let's go." He doesn't know how to say no, and he doesn't even think about his responsibilities.

We've been together for three years, a year before we moved in together. Before we even started going out, we knew each other, and his drinking was pretty bad then. He already went away once for treatment for 45 days but it didn't help. Now he says sometimes, "I should go to treatment for 30 days."

When he mentions it, I agree, but then he says, "I wouldn't see the girls for 30 days."

I tell him, "That's better than you drinking all the time."

Elaine, 19/Antonio, 17 (Kianna, 13 months; Sarah, 2 months)

Antonio has already been in treatment for 45 days and he's currently going to AA (Alcoholics Anonymous) meetings. Only 17, he has a pattern of heavy drinking for three years already. It's not easy to stop.

An addicted person is unlikely to be able to commit fully to another person.

For many teens, it's not simply alcohol or drugs. It's a mixture, which often makes it even harder to stop.

If your partner is drinking too much or is taking drugs, his/her ability to communicate with you and capacity for intimacy have probably decreased, perhaps greatly. That's hard to understand. An addicted person is unlikely to be able to commit fully to another person.

If either of you has a drug or alcohol problem, it's important that you both get counseling. An addicted person is not going to get over that addiction without help.

Attending Alcoholics Anonymous meetings has helped
many people quit drinking.

Alcoholics Anonymous and Narcotics Anonymous are
good resources. AA groups differ, so if you or your partner
goes to a group and it doesn't seem helpful, try another
one. If you're a teen and you go to a group composed
mostly of elderly people, for example, you probably won't
get the help you want. Find a group that fits your needs.

What Can a Partner Do?

If you're the partner of an addicted person, you need to
figure out how to take care of yourself first. You need to
learn to cope with the reality of what's going on. Start with
Alanon which provides help for partners and other relatives
of alcoholics. Go by yourself if you can't get your partner
to go. You have to know whether you are unwittingly
encouraging your partner's addiction. You need to learn

how to be supportive without taking responsibility for your mate's problems.

Alanon and AA often have groups for young people. An important reason to get involved is to find a role model, someone who has been through what you're experiencing, and has found a way to recover.

Know that the addicted person will slip—but must try again. It will be a life-long battle.

Help from the Community of Hope

Bud Christenson, pastor of the Sheridan Lutheran Church, Lincoln, Nebraska, is deeply involved in helping young people with such problems as alcoholism and drug addiction through the church's Community of Hope program. Community of Hope is a non-profit organization in Lincoln in which several churches participate.

Sheridan Lutheran's program is designed to help people help each other. It's a peer-helping organization, somewhat like AA. As an example, Pastor Christenson described their newest clients, a couple coming off the streets asking for help. Both are recovering alcoholics, each has earned a GED (General Equivalency Diploma), and they have a baby. Their families have given up and no longer will help them.

"I'll start looking for unskilled labor opportunities for them today. Hopefully, we'll have the two of them working, and we'll get them some child care, some clothes, and a haircut," Pastor Christenson said.

"I told them, 'We'll walk with you and we'll be your friends.' They need a substitute for family when the family is not there.

"The Community of Hope meets every Thursday night. We meet and tell each other our stories. 'What's happening? How did the job interview go? Have you been sober for a week?' They help each other.

"It takes a very, very strong commitment, and there are a lot of ups and downs in recovery," he commented. "Mostly, helping takes a lot of tough love, picking them up when they fall."

Know you really can't do it for your partner.
You can do it only for yourself.

Pastor Christenson cautioned people who are trying to help a partner overcome an addiction. "It would be very unusual for a partner to be able to provide all the needed help," he said. "You need to encourage your mate to seek help as quickly as possible. Know you really can't do it for your partner. You can do it only for yourself.

"Partners, of course, can be an important part of the individual's recovery. We focus on helping the partners be all they can be. We encourage them to

• stop harping at the partner.
• stop trying to cover up for the partner.
• concentrate on being gentle and honest.

"It won't be easy," he stressed.

Finding the Help You Need

"Put in your book where you go to get help," Trina urged, then added, "I'm not the type to find help. I want help to come to me, so I'm mostly alone with my problems."

It's hard for people to help if they don't know you need help, as Trina has learned. If you or your partner has an addiction—and are willing to look for help—start with the phone book. Look for Alcoholics Anonymous, a widely used recovery program for people who drink too much. Alanon is for family members of alcoholics. Narcotics

Anonymous, as the name implies, is for those addicted to narcotics.

If you don't find the number you want in your directory, call Alanon, 1/800/344-2666, and ask for a local number.

If you'd like to find something similar to Pastor Christenson's Community of Hope, check out the churches in your area. "There will be a church somewhere that can help," he said. "Keep your ear to the ground, and you'll hear about it."

Valerie and Martin—The Road to Recovery

Valerie and Martin's story demonstrates the development of addiction and the difficult road to recovery:

We moved into our own apartment when Braxton was about 7 months old. Martin had been drinking quite heavily and I wasn't aware of the problem. The money would disappear, and I didn't know where it went. He'd watch the baby in the evening and I had a part-time job.

For the longest time I didn't want anybody to know about it. I tried to hide it. I did everything I could to make everybody think everything was fine. This went on for so long, I couldn't do it any more. I do have this bad self-conscious thing that we aren't very old, we have two children, and people look at us funny. I was afraid if people knew about it, they might take our kids.

He finally realized he had a problem.

Martin's money would go to drugs, and going out partying with his buddies. One time he got a new job, and was getting pretty good money. He said we'd go out to a bar and get a drink. But he came home at

*9:30, after getting off at 3, and he had $50. That
wouldn't pay the rent. That wouldn't even buy diapers. That's when it hit. Something had to change.*

*We talked to our pastor. He came over one day and
said, "We're going to have this group, and I'd like
you to be there." Martin said okay, although he didn't
know what it would be.*

*We went to the group. They were discussing
chronic drinking, and it hit him. He finally realized he
had a problem . . . a month later, he agreed to go
away to a treatment center. I think it's helping him.*

*I'm doing things like being with the young mothers
group, Alanon — I have to realize your support group
doesn't have to be family. I've gotten a little wiser as
my sons get older, and I've gotten more determined.*

*Where Martin is, he's working on his anger prob-
lem. He had been holding a lot of that in, and he's
learning how to deal with this without drinking. They
are also teaching him responsibility. He has to pay
rent there, he has to have a job.*

*When he went there he had to go to an AA meeting
every night. Now he's down to four a week. He works
at a car wash, and he's setting some goals for himself
when he gets out. We'll have to stay on some assistance. He'll work and go to school part-time.*

*When he gets out we'll continue the Community of
Hope group. We'll set some goals. No matter what,
I'll continue school. I'm in an academic transfer
program. I'll be at Community College for a year,
then transfer to the University. I want to be a nurse.*

*My biggest thing is to have a support system. The
couple needs to work together. It has to be a team
support with a lot of cooperation and communication.*

Valerie, 22/Martin, 21 (Braxton, 4; Kyle, 14 months)

A few days after Martin came home from the treatment center, he talked about his history of addiction:

I was doing drugs a lot back then. I was young and didn't have any responsibilities. I quit school in tenth grade, but I'm going back this spring.

When we got our own apartment, we felt free. I was drinking then. I had just turned 17 when Valerie had the baby, and the only way I could cope with it was with drinking, having a baby that young. I don't think I was ready for it. I needed something.

Things got bad then, and I said, "I'll quit drinking," and things got better again. I guess I figured since things were getting better, it wouldn't hurt to do some drugs. So I was substituting one for the other. I cut the alcohol totally and went straight to drugs.

Oh man, things were bad. I tried them off and on since I was 13, but when it started getting intense was probably two years ago. I like to do a little of hallucinogenic drugs, LSD and marijuana—a temporary release from reality. I had good times when I was high, but they caused me nothing but trouble.

Things weren't going right. It was like hitting rock bottom. Basically I just got tired of being sick and tired. It was coming to a point I was going to lose my family. Either the drugs or my family, and I chose my family. I went to treatment for 26 days.

> I decided I'd go ahead and get the help I needed. I was by myself— no one else could do it for me.

It was hard to deal with responsibility. I'm slowly getting my priorities straight now. It has taken about

*three months to realize that. I want to go to school,
and I want to become a police officer. I think it's time
to grow up and move on. I can't let Valerie leave me
behind.*

*I work on emotional feelings now. There was a lack
of communication, and that's something I need to
look at, to help me and help my family. I've bottled up
my emotions too much, and I need to get those out so
I don't go in relapse. I'm trying hard to show my
emotions. I don't cry, but I try to share things with
Valerie. There has to be some kind of trust and
honesty. Things can only get better.*

*I'm very grateful that I still have Valerie and the
kids, and that I decided I'd go ahead and get the help
I needed. I was by myself—no one else could do it for
me. It makes me proud of myself now. When you use,
you have low self-esteem.*

*Four months ago our life was a total disaster.
There could have been only one other conclusion
besides losing my family, and that was death.*

Martin

The future looks much better for Martin and Valerie.
Martin understands he will always be "in recovery." If he
starts drinking or doing drugs again, he's likely to get into
trouble very soon. He plans to stay clean.

Dealing—Not for Dads

Jeremiah used to be a drug dealer. Candi feels her
encouragement helped him stop:

*When we first were together, he was selling drugs.
I told him we were having a baby now, and he had to
let all that go. He stopped selling drugs and got more
involved with me when I was pregnant.*

> *It was hard for him to get used to just a paycheck,*
> *but now he accepts it, and he wouldn't go back to*
> *dealing. He changed because he realized he had a*
> *family, and he didn't want to lose his family.*
>
> Candi, 20/Jeremiah, 21 (Jakela, 2; Kamika, 1)

Jeremiah, too, commented on his past dealing and the reasons he stopped:

> *I'm not outside all the time any more. I mostly*
> *have new friends. The old friends, life style with no*
> *kids, not settled down, not with the same girl or the*
> *same guy, and I can't keep up with that.*
>
> *I left drug selling—I can't handle that. I did it for*
> *one year. I was seeing my friends going to jail and*
> *understanding it was wrong, and you could spend the*
> *rest of your life in jail for doing it, so I swayed away.*
> *It wasn't overnight—it took a year, but I got away.*
>
> Jeremiah

The important thing here is that Jeremiah no longer is a dealer. He's working, supporting his family, and finding life with Candi, Jakela, and Kamika is a good choice.

Helping Each Other

"The really important thing that young people (and all of us) need to learn," Pastor Christenson added, "is that life is about helping each other. You don't really know what recovery is about until you start living for the other person, until you start caring about the other person's well-being."

If you or your partner is addicted to drugs or alcohol, find help quickly. Get into a recovery program. Set goals for yourselves, and get on with your life together. Nobody says it will be easy, but it's the only way you can win.

If you're being abused, GET OUT—
for your children's sake as well as your own.

CHAPTER 10

People Are
Not for Hitting

When he hit me, I didn't do anything about it for at least two years. We were living at his parents, and it was hard. I was barely 14. I had known him for about a month when I started dating him, and then I moved in with him.

When I started living with Manuel, everything seemed to be all right. He used drugs, but I didn't know. Then he became jealous and he started hitting me, and I didn't do nothing about it.

I saw my parents twice during those two years because he didn't let me come over. I was upset, but I couldn't do anything because he'd hit me. So I'd say "All right, I'm not going."

He wouldn't let me go to school. He'd say I would be with somebody else.

*Then when I got pregnant I decided I didn't want
to be with him because of my baby. I've had a bad
life. I'm with my parents now.*

Lourdes, 16/Manuel, 15 (Katrina, 4 months)

*Sam pushed me once, and I said that's one thing
I'm not going to take. I said if he ever pushed me
again or hit me, I wouldn't be with him. He apologized, and he stopped. He said, "I don't know what
came over me. I'd never hit you. I don't know why I
pushed you."*

*Plus the way he'd talk to me. He'd cuss and call
me names. I'd just look at him and say, "I don't talk
to you like that. I think you should give me the respect
I give you."*

*I don't know what guys start thinking when they
think they can just control you and yell at you. It's not
right. I told him it's not. We had a speaker at school
about domestic violence, and I brought the papers
home. We read them together.*

*But I had to change, too. I was hitting him and
calling him "Stupid."*

*My mom said, "You're doing the same thing."
I said, "No, I'm not."*

"Read the papers," she said. I did, and I was.

*It made me think. Why would I do it to him if I
didn't want him to hit me? He'd just take it. He
wouldn't say anything, and we'd make up and
everything would be fine.*

Neither of us hits now.

Myra, 17/Sam, 18

Extent of the Problem

One-third to one-half of all American women are, at
some time, beaten by their husbands or lovers. Somewhere

in the United States a woman is battered every 15 seconds by her husband, boyfriend, or live-in partner, according to the National Coalition Against Domestic Violence.

There is still an alarming acceptance of partner abuse. In our Marriage Expectations Survey, we asked respondents how they feel about a man hitting his partner. One in five of the 830 males said it was either okay, sometimes necessary, or may happen when he's angry or drunk. Among the 2898 females responding, a few said it was okay (less than 1 percent), 3 percent said it's sometimes necessary, and 10 percent agreed it may happen when he's angry or drunk.

The good news is that these percentages are significantly lower than they were ten years ago when we did a similar survey. The bad news is that many young people still condone a man hitting his partner.

Problem Much More Severe for Women

People are *not* for hitting, whether male or female. The problem is much more severe for women, however, simply because of their size and strength as compared to men. For most couples, the man is bigger and can hit harder than the woman. From a physical standpoint, if she hits him, he can stop her. But she can't stop him.

Partner abuse is a problem
for women of all ages,
but even more so for teenage women.

Among the 588 teen women living with a partner and responding to the above survey, 42 percent said their partner had hit them at least once. More than one in ten said he had hit her five or more times. Of the 67 teen men in the survey who lived with a partner, 30 percent admitted to hitting their partner at least once, 6 percent, five or more times.

I have worked with pregnant and parenting teens for 20 years, and I've talked with many young women who have been abused by their partners. When I was teaching, students occasionally explained their absence from class by saying they didn't want the other girls to see them with a black eye.

Partner abuse is a problem for women of all ages, but even more so for teenage women. A young woman who hasn't yet found her self-identity may be a prime target for an abusive partner relationship. This is even more likely to happen if early pregnancy and parenting reinforce her feelings of dependence.

It's Hard to Walk Out

One day we were showing the movie, "The Burning Bed," a story of an abused woman. About half-way through the movie, a student rushed out of the classroom in tears. I followed her, knowing her partner was abusive, and concerned that the movie had made her feel even worse.

As she stood outside crying, she said, "They think leaving is easy. They don't understand. I can't leave him . . ." She had heard a couple of the other students talking about her situation, and she simply couldn't handle it.

If you have a friend who is being abused by her partner, you probably wonder why she doesn't leave him. But, whatever your age, if you're the victim of abuse, you *know* how hard it is to walk out, to face life on your own. You may think you deserve the abuse, which makes it even harder to get out.

James has a bad temper. Little things I'd say set him off. The hitting began when I lived with him the first time, but it wasn't that bad, just a slap here and a slap there. It started happening when I was about 6 months pregnant. He wanted to go out and I wouldn't want him to, and he would slap me. Then after I moved out, he'd hit me maybe once a month at his house when I'd spend the weekend with him.

We moved out together, and we thought it would be real fun because we had our own apartment. Then little by little he started hitting me again until he was hitting me a lot. When he'd hit me, I'd cry.

People ask, "Why didn't you fight back?"

My first reaction was, "How could he hurt me like this?" I'd just cry. Sometimes the baby was there. Half the time he was sleeping.

I kept thinking James would change.
He'd say, "I'm real sorry,"
and then he'd do it again.

Once he was violent to Jacari. James was baby-sitting him while I was working in the summer. I trusted him because this was his son. We picked Jacari up from James one day, and the baby had a black eye. I was in shock.

The best thing to do is to get out of the relationship. It's not easy. It took me a long time. You just have to keep telling yourself you can make it, that you will find someone better, or maybe you don't even want someone else, you can make it on your own. Now I realize that my son comes first.

How do you decide when it's time to leave? I decided it wasn't right for my son. Everybody was telling me it wasn't right for him to see us arguing, that it would affect him later on, and I decided that was right. And I was tired of not being able to say what I thought because I would get hit, or if I didn't want to do what he wanted me to do, I'd get hit.

*My whole life was being destroyed because of that.
I wasn't doing good in school or anything. I kept
thinking James would change. He would say he
wouldn't do it any more, "I'm real sorry," and then
he'd do it again.*

*Then I met this person before we split. He's a real,
real nice person, and I thought, "Wow, I can have
this instead of him."*

                                        Angelica, 18 (Jacari, 3 years)

Hopefully Angelica would have split whether or not she
"met this nice person." Staying in an abusive situation is
surely worse than being alone.

A 16-year-old in our Teen Parent Program broke up with
her boyfriend recently. She had said that he occasionally hit
her. I commented that breaking up sounded like a good
move for her, but that I knew it took strength on her part.

"Not especially," she replied. "I have a new boyfriend. I
met him just in time."

In other words, she had to have a boyfriend.

Wanting to be with a partner is a normal human emotion
shared by many people. Having to be with a partner because you can't cope without him, however, can be dangerous. If you are in an abusive relationship, get out. You will
learn to cope without him.

Victor and Trina live together but are not yet married.
Victor thinks being married would allow him to hit Trina:

*Sometimes I feel like hitting her, but I go outside or
something. I have no right to be hitting Trina.*

*If we were married, I'd have more right to hit her
because she would be married to me.*

                                Victor, 16/Trina, 16 (Felipe, 3 1/2 months)

Marriage absolutely is *not* a license for hitting. *No one
deserves abuse.* No one deserves to be pushed, slapped, or
ridiculed. No one deserves to be spied on or isolated. If

your partner hits or slaps you, you're being abused. The abuse must stop—or you must leave.

If you're not in an abusive situation and never have been, keep it that way!

> *No hitting. Eric told me it don't make him much of a man if he has to hit on a woman. But I wouldn't let him hit me in the first place.*
>
> Jonitha, 17/Eric, 22 (Denae, 1 year)

Finding the Courage to Leave

Jessica and Brad were only 14 when Brad moved in with Jessica and her mother. He stayed for 1 1/2 years. Jessica described the changes occurring in their relationship, and how she finally realized she could survive without Brad. For a long time, she thought she had no choice:

> *I guess I was too young to get involved in the first place. At first he seemed so wonderful. I didn't think he would ever be able to hit me.*
>
> *We were 14 when he moved in, and I felt like I needed to be with him all the time. At first we got along good. Then within about six months he wouldn't let me wear make-up or go out with my friends. All I could wear was sweats because he didn't want me showing off my body.*
>
> *He was really jealous. I couldn't talk on the phone unless he was on the other line listening to everything I said.*
>
> *He always bad-mouthed me in front of his friends and in front of my friends because he had to feel he was in control. For awhile I didn't have my friends because I couldn't go out with them because of him.*
>
> *I could talk with them at school but that was all. When I told them, it helped, but they just said, "You should leave. You should get out of the relationship."*

One time when I tried to end the relationship, if he couldn't have me, he said nobody could. I knew he had access to guns. It was real frightening.

He's been gone about two months. He was always emotionally abusive to me. He called me these terrible, terrible things, and I would cry and cry. I guess the reason he turned to physical abuse was because I just tuned him out.

When I was with him, I had nobody else to talk with. I didn't know any better. I didn't know I could get another boyfriend. I didn't realize I could go out with my friends and have fun, and have fun without a boyfriend. He was my first boyfriend.

I would think, "I have the baby now and what would I do out on my own?" I didn't think I could make it by myself.

I know I can make it on my own now. I think I just had enough. When I saw him treat our son the way he did, that was a big turning point. I thought if he can abuse me, some day he's going to abuse Rodney, and Rodney doesn't deserve it. I know Brad's mom was abusive to them also, but I don't want that to carry through to my son. Brad never knew his father.

Now I know the signs to look for. At first Brad would just tell me, "You look better without make-up." Then if I put it on, he would say, "What did I tell you?" He was very jealous.

Jessica, 15/Brad, 15 (Rodney, 4 months)

Jessica explained another concern:

Once after we split up, he came over to see Rodney. Brad was so rough with him, he didn't handle him right, and Rodney never did anything to Brad. He is still trying to control me by saying he will shoot Rodney if I leave the house.

*"I didn't realize I could go out with my friends
and have fun without a boyfriend."*

*I haven't seen Brad for six weeks. But he finds
ways. He calls. He won't say anything, but I know
who he is. It's scary. I know if something happened to
me, he would have rights to the baby.*

Jessica is probably right in thinking Brad "has rights to
the baby" if she has done nothing to change his legal rights.
She needs to go to court and ask to have Brad's custody
and visitation rights removed. She probably has enough
evidence to do so. She should check with Legal Aid.

Battering Compared to Rape

Partner abuse is much like rape. Rape, of course, is not a
crime of sex, it's a crime of violence. Partner-beating is
also a crime of violence.

Society's attitudes toward both crimes have been similar.
Too often, it has been assumed the rape victim did something to bring on the attack. It must have been because of

the way she dressed or the way she walked. In the same vein, women who are beaten by their partners run into this kind of thinking. "You must have done something to make him hit you."

> *It was about three months after we started living together that he started hitting me. I was scared.*
> *It was hard. I'd be scared but I accepted it. I never said anything. It was like I let him do it, like I gave him permission, like I thought that was what made him happy. He hit more and more often.*
>
> Arkameia, 18/Joshua, 20 (Erica, 13 months)

Arkameia finally left Joshua. Joshua is now in jail, and she is sure they will not be together again.

If you are in an abusive situation,
either the abuse must stop
or you must get out!

A person who feels guilty herself because her husband or lover hit her is not likely to leave him. She doesn't feel good enough about herself to be able to take that step. Often she feels embarrassed, damaged. She thinks she must have done something wrong. If she didn't do something wrong, she must *not* have done something she was supposed to do.

Nothing excuses either rape or partner abuse. No one deserves to be hit just as no one deserves to be raped. If you are in an abusive situation, either the abuse must stop or you *must* get out!

Desperate Need for Women's Shelters

Battered women often have no place to go except back to their husbands or partners. For this reason, many

communities have established shelters for battered women
and their children. Usually a woman may stay there as long
as 30 days. Counseling and other services are provided
as needed.

Most women who go into a shelter have nothing but the
clothes they're wearing—and their kids. The house, the car,
the bank account are still with the husband. What can they
do? They don't have money to get into an apartment. Often
they don't have jobs. If they don't have a car, it's hard to
get to work. It's difficult to get to the store.

Often they go back home, only to be beaten again.

You might think nothing can change in only 30 days in a
shelter. However, the shelter's goal is likely to be to help
women gain "psychological empowerment" for themselves.
This means the counselors try to help each woman understand that she is important, that she has a right not to be
beaten. Battered women generally have very low
self-esteem.

Only by thinking badly of herself could a woman convince herself that she deserves such treatment. But she can
be helped to understand her own worth, that she is a

dreams are lost

all my dreams were dashed the day you hit me
all my hopes were halted by your hate
all my love dissolved in your denials
all my faith faltered by your fist

there are no dreams left for me to give you
i've lost whatever hope of us i had
i have no strength to hold us both together
violence wins again and dreams are lost.

By Mary Marecek, *Breaking Free from Partner Abuse*, p. 41

valuable person, and that no one has a right to physically
assault her. Only then does she have a chance at taking
control of her life. Only then will she be able to become
strong enough to stay away from the partner who abused
her. Only then does she have a chance at developing job
skills and finding a job to support herself and her children.

Which Men Batter?

There are bound to be tensions and disagreements in any
relationship between two people. Some men respond with
violence. They may think they have a right to do so. Sometimes a man thinks of his wife as property.

How can you tell if a man is likely to beat you? We
know men who batter their wives represent all ethnic
groups. We know some are very poor, but others have good
jobs with high incomes. Men who beat their wives often
say, afterward, that they love their women.

Was he physically or psychologically abused as a child
or did his father abuse his mother? If so, he's likely to
repeat the pattern by abusing his partner.

Statistically, this is the single most important thing in
wife-beating—that the man's mother was beaten by his
father. This has been compared to the fact that, if your
parents speak English, you will also speak English. This is
the language you learned from them.

If your father beat your mother you are likely, if you are
a man, to beat your wife. If you are a woman, you are likely
to think that is the way life is.

Does he act in a violent way toward other people? Does
he lose his temper more often than seems necessary? Does
he damage things, such as putting his fist through the door,
throwing things, or destroying property such as clothing?

Does he drink too much alcohol?

Is he extremely jealous? Does he expect you to spend all

your free time with him? And if you aren't with him, does he insist on knowing exactly where you are?

Does he feel strongly that men and women should act according to traditional sex-role stereotypes?

If you see any of these characteristics in the person with whom you're considering marriage or living together, proceed with caution. Once a pattern of violence is started, it's extremely hard to stop.

Van Freemon, who helped establish the Women's Crisis Center in Whittier, California, described a common situation: "When a battered woman comes into our Crisis Center, I ask, 'When did he start beating you?'

"She will say, 'About six months ago.'

"Then I ask, 'When was the first time he hit you?'

"They've been married six years, and she answers, 'Six months after we were married.'

"I'll say, 'But you just said he started six months ago.'

"'Oh, that's the first time he put me in the hospital.' She didn't think he was beating her if she didn't have to be hospitalized! That's a lot of denial."

Hitting is abuse from the *first* time it happens.

Three-Stage Cycle Is Typical

Lenore E. Walker, author of *The Battered Woman* (1982: HarperCollins), describes a three-stage cycle followed by men who batter their partners. The first phase she calls the "Tension-Building Phase."

Tension mounts in the relationship. The woman learns to recognize signs that the cycle is starting again. He becomes more and more irritable. He can't cope with everyday stress.

She will do anything possible not to annoy him during this stage. But that doesn't help because she isn't to blame. It is not her fault. His problem is within himself.

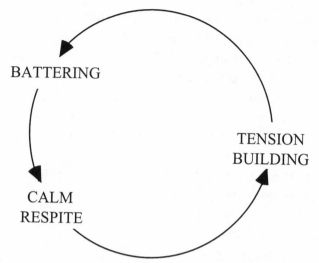

The next phase is the "Battering Incident." At first, the batterer wants only to teach the victim a lesson. He doesn't mean to inflict injury, but in the process, he loses control of his rage. Only he can end this stage.

Sometimes a woman can guess about when this stage will end, and she leaves home until it's safe to return. She needs a place to hide during this phase. Once it's over, the victim often denies the seriousness of her injuries and the reality that this can happen again—and again.

The third stage Ms. Walker terms "Calm Respite." He becomes extremely kind and loving. He apologizes. He's afraid she will leave, so he becomes a charming model mate. Both try to convince themselves that everything will be okay from now on.

But then his inner tension begins to build again, finally to be released through another assault on his partner. The cycle is never-ending unless he is helped by expert counseling.

"Once a pattern of violence is started in a relationship, it almost always gets worse. He beats her more often, or more severely, or both. A battered woman lives in terror of her next beating because she knows she may not live through it," Ms. Freemon explained.

> *A lot of people ask, "Why didn't you just leave?"*
> *One day I woke up in the hospital from Bernie, and I knew it was time. My friends came, and said, "We didn't think you'd wake up."*
>
> *Throughout the whole time they tried to get me to walk away from him, and I always said, "I can't." I was with him for three years. I was 12 and he was 14. I couldn't believe that we were that young and he was that way already.*
>
> *His mother didn't want him so his grandmother raised him. He always resented his mom, and I think he resents the world. He always had a chip on his shoulder.*
>
> Tiffany, 18 (Keosha, 11 months)

Tiffany is now married to Shaun, 19, and it's a much different kind of relationship. She explained:

> *When I first met Shaun, I was really afraid abuse would happen again. I told him my other boyfriend hit me, and Shaun watched what he did and what he said so it wouldn't worry me.*
>
> *It takes a lot to make Shaun angry. We have fights, but we never go to bed angry.*
>
> *When we started going out, I made sure there'd be no hitting. In my other relationship, Bernie had to control everything I did. With Shaun, it was "I'm not going to hold you back from doing anything."*

Counseling May Help

> *Alfonso hit me in the face once when I was pregnant. I told him to get out and don't ever come back. He left, and I threw his stuff outside.*

He was gone for maybe a week. Then he called and said he would never do it again. I said, "You aren't going to hit me again, or you won't be part of my life any longer."

Arlene, 14/Alfonso, 16 (Sylvia, 4 months)

Usually two things must happen to stop an abusive relationship:

1. The woman must make it clear that she will not accept the violence any longer, and the man must believe she means it.

2. The abuser must get counseling.

Meghan talked about the abuse she had received from Justin, and how they're trying to work things out:

Things didn't really build up until several months after we had our own place and the bills kept coming, and we didn't have any free time. If we did, the baby was there. Then we went to counseling, but only once because we never had time for more. We both tried, but it was just too much. And one evening it got violent and I moved out.

He had hit me once before. No way will I put up with that. I'm nobody's punching bag. He has done everything. He has apologized. He has enrolled in a class for men who abuse women.

We continue to date. He sees the baby. We go out on weekends together. He wants me to come back, but I'm not ready for that. I have told him he has a lot of things to work on and so do I. We need some space away from each other, I guess.

He's going to counseling, and soon we'll go together.

He started college, but right now he's trying to save enough money to go back. I graduate high school in

June, and I have already registered for college. Jameka is old enough for the college child care center.

I really don't know what's going to happen. We've discussed what we'd do if we broke up, and we've decided if we do, it will be on friendly terms because of our baby.

I definitely know I'm going to college for four years, do the best I can to get a good education for my son and myself.

Meghan, 18/Justin, 21 (Jameka, 2 1/2 years)

Meghan and Justin may be able to work out their problems. They are doing several positive things:

- Meghan made it clear she would be "nobody's punching bag."
- Justin realizes he has a problem, and is in a group for men who abuse women.
- Meghan and Justin plan to get counseling together.
- Both Meghan and Justin are continuing their education and career preparation, an important part of building self-esteem. Two people with high self-esteem are less likely to express frustration through violence.

If you or someone you know is in an abusive relationship, professional help is needed. Some well-trained counselors may still be in the "It must be her fault" mind-set. This is certainly not the kind of counseling designed to help the woman get out of a dangerous situation or to get the man into counseling. Calling a Women's Center for referrals is the best approach.

Staying in a shelter can give a woman a little time for counseling and help in planning for her future. She may decide to leave her partner permanently. Or she may decide to reconcile with him after he accepts counseling.

Whatever the situation, *people are not for hitting!*

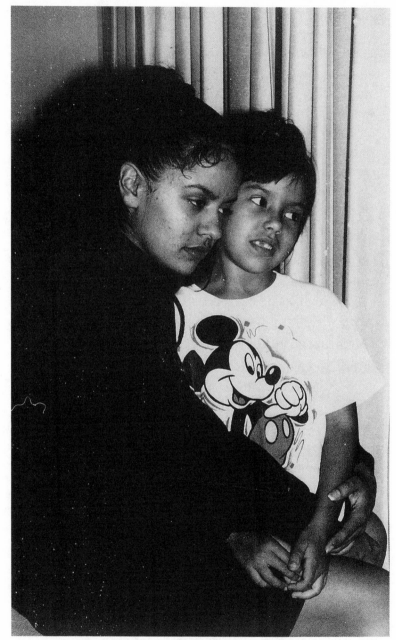

Sometimes divorce is the best decision,
but it's still difficult for everyone involved.

CHAPTER 11

Sometimes
A Relationship Ends

*Before André moved in, we got along. Basically I
didn't know that much about him. A lot of the things
he did that were the reasons we broke up, he did
secretly before he moved in.*

*At first it was okay. It was kind of fun because I
could have him around, and we could talk and stuff.
But after awhile he wasn't coming home as often. He
was constantly out with his friends. I'd ask him to
watch the baby and he'd say no, he was doing something else. We started fighting, and we broke up.*

*Be very realistic. It's all well and fine to think the
person is going to stay with you forever, but take it
one day at a time and be realistic. If I had known then
what I know now, I wouldn't have been with André.*

Desiree, 18 (Keisha, 4 months)

We lived together for four years. It was good for about two years, and then . . . I thought about counseling, but it was the money thing. Seamus is still involved with our child. Both of us have custody, and we still talk to each other. No legal work was done.

Lila, 21 (Laura, 2 years)

How does one decide when to give up on a relationship? Most of us want marriage to be forever. We want a perfect marriage where nothing will ever go wrong. But as far as I know, no one has ever found that perfect relationship.

It Won't Be Easy

A comment I heard often from teenage couples was, "Too many people expect it to be easy. They think the first little thing that goes wrong means splitting up."

This book has two purposes. One is to help young people not yet married make a wise decision concerning this big step in their lives. An even more important purpose is to help young people already married or living together develop an even better relationship than they have now—or at least to suggest some ways of working together on problem areas in their relationship.

But not all relationships last. At least 60 percent of teenagers who marry divorce within five years. An even higher percentage of living-together couples split up. Most of these young people, no doubt, expected their relationships to last. In the beginning, they probably said, "It won't happen to us. We're in love, and we'll work out our problems and have a wonderful life together." But time after time it doesn't happen. Many young couples who thought marriage was their answer are no longer together.

Just as every person is different, so is every couple's relationship unique. No two couples are exactly alike, but sometimes we can learn from another person's experience.

Many of us expect marriage to solve problems. "He'll change after we're married." Or "She'll settle down once we're married." This is not a given. Living with a partner does not necessarily make one a more responsible or a better person.

Difference in Values May Destroy Love

Matai was 16 when she married Jay. He was 21. They had known each other four months. She was not pregnant until several months after they married.

Several things went wrong. Because he was 21, five years older than she, he was always "in charge." She also realized they were far apart in their values, in what they wanted out of life. They had very little in common. She shared her story:

Before we got married, he treated me half-way decent. They say love is blind, and I guess I couldn't see what he was like. I partied with him a lot, but I quit after we got married. But he never stopped. He'd be out drinking, and I'd be sitting up half the night waiting. I don't think that's the way marriage is supposed to be.

> All along I pretty much knew
> he wasn't treating me right,
> but he wasn't willing to change.

After we were married, he started treating me like property rather than as a human being. My sister overheard him tell his brother that a wife is supposed to have the house clean, his shoes by the door, give him a hug when he comes in, then go to bed with him! He was always smoking pot and drinking, and I mean every day. That's where our money went. He said he made the money, and I didn't have anything to do with how it was spent.

We were together only a few months when his brother and his wife moved in. Jay didn't even talk to me about it. They just moved in. They'd mess up the house and I was supposed to keep it clean. But I was pregnant, and I was trying to go to school. Sometimes on Sundays they had a big barbecue and they were very messy. I'd go to bed, then go to school the next day. After school I'd come home and clean up the mess.

I kept trying to make it work, but he didn't. I kept talking to him about straightening up his act, and he said that was the way he was. If I didn't like it, I should leave. All along I pretty much knew he wasn't treating me right, but he wasn't willing to change.

I didn't put my foot down until after little Quint was born. A week after we had him, Jay wanted to take Quint over to his friend's house. They would all be smoking and drinking, so I told him no. For a week, we didn't talk. Before, I had always done what Jay said, but this time I didn't. It really shocked him, and about a week later he walked out on us.

Then a few days later I called him, and he came back. He said he would straighten up his act, but he lied. I think he came back for sexual reasons—you know how men are—but he stayed only two weeks, then walked out again. I filed for divorce after that.

His Reality Is Different

Of course this is an account of Matai's "reality." Jay saw their life together in a very different way:

Sure, I like to party, but I wasn't "always" drunk or high like Matai claims. I thought she liked a good time, too. She changed after we got married. She just stayed home—especially after she got pregnant.

I suppose I should have realized she was just too young. All she could think about was going to school, coming home, and sitting here. Man, I'd go crazy with that life.

Her parents were always there, taking care of her. But she didn't want anything to do with my family. My brother and his wife drove in one day from Nebraska. I didn't know they were coming, and they needed a place to live quick. We were having trouble paying our bills, so I thought Matai would appreciate them sharing expenses. But no, she almost had a coronary.

They both found jobs right away. I thought, since Matai got home from school two hours before we got off work, she could clean up the house and get supper. She didn't see it my way.

Then when Quint was born, I couldn't believe her. She was really paranoid. I wanted to take the baby over to see a friend of mine, and she absolutely refused. Yes, I did walk out. I need to have some say-so in my own home.

Lots of problems here—but basically it was a marriage of two very different and very young people. Matai offered some helpful final advice:

You should know the person a longer time. I only knew Jay for four months. I had dated only one other person. It's probably better to find out more about other people in the world rather than just settling down young. Just try to keep your eyes open. If there are things about him you don't like, do you want to put up with that the rest of your life?

I guess I was pretty blind before we were married.

Quick Divorce Not Always the Answer

If you and your partner have no hope that you can make it as a couple, it's probably better to know that now and get on with your lives. However, a tremendous number of people at all age levels today cut out too quickly. They think their marriage won't work, so they get a divorce.

Sometimes it's better to try to work things out, to realize that both of you probably contribute to the bad situation. Look at the things that brought you two together. What attracted you to each other in the first place? Are these things still there, and are they worth saving? What do you still have to give to each other?

Both people have to work at their relationship if it is to be successful. Sometimes it takes professional counseling. A lot of today's divorces could probably be prevented.

If you aren't yet married, ask yourself, "What do I want from marriage?" Ask your partner the same question. What do you have to give to each other? Why do you think this marriage would work? One thing is sure. If you want a "forever" marriage, you both have to work at it—forever.

Professional Counseling Might Help

If you and your partner are having problems, problems you don't seem to be solving on your own, perhaps professional counseling would help.

Sometimes people feel they "shouldn't" need a counselor—only crazy people can't solve their own problems. Or a couple may think if they can't get along very well, it's nobody else's business.

We've talked about counseling, but neither of us really wants to go. If we can't work out our own problems, how can some other person help us?

Lena, 17/Guy, 19

Most people are willing to see a doctor if they break a leg or get a bad case of the flu. If they have a legal problem, they may find a good lawyer to advise them.

In the same way, a professional counselor can help an ailing marriage. Rather, the counselor can help you and your partner figure out how, through working together, you two can help your marriage improve. It's certainly not a shameful thing to see a counselor. People who do so are willing to admit they have a problem and that they would like to solve that problem.

If you want to find a counselor, ask your friends or your doctor for recommendations. Perhaps your pastor, priest or rabbi could help you. Try to find someone who appears to be knowledgable about counseling. The person you see should be credentialed in your state as a psychologist, clinical social worker, or a marriage and family counselor.

It's best to get the names of three or four highly recommended people, then call each one and ask some questions. How long does the therapist expect the counseling to continue? You probably aren't looking for years of therapy. Three or four sessions might help, or you might find you and your partner need ten or twelve appointments.

Ask about fees, and learn whether or not your health insurance will cover the charges. Does the counselor see you and your spouse separately or together? A good counselor will probably want both individual appointments and couple appointments.

If you think you and your spouse need a counselor but your spouse refuses to go with you, what should you do? Ask the counselor's opinion. Usually they much prefer to see both persons, but are willing to see only one when necessary.

You can't change your spouse directly, and if your partner won't see the counselor with you, you may think

A counselor may be able to help you problem-solve.

it's an impossible situation. But you may be surprised. The counselor may help you understand your situation so much better that, even if your partner isn't getting counseling with you, s/he will profit from your experience.

If There's Violence

Belen and Rafael lived together for a year. After Belen got pregnant, Rafael became much more jealous. He didn't "allow" Belen to see her friends. He started hitting her. Finally Belen found the strength to break away. She is firm about the need to leave if you're being hit:

If you're in this kind of situation, don't think you're stuck just because you have a baby. You can do it on your own. You don't have to have a man there to help you. Don't be dependent on him because he may not

always be there. Stay in school and do the best you
can. Don't give up no matter how hard it gets.

Rafael cared a lot, I know he did, but I didn't like
his possessiveness and his violence. I hated it. I
stayed with him because I loved him and I still do, but
no matter how much you love a person, if they hit
you—nobody should be treated like that.

So many people think they can't split because they
have the baby and they need the guy. They think they
can't do it on their own, but it's always possible.
Once the hitting starts, don't excuse it for anything,
because once he does it, it will never stop. There will
always be another time for it.

When he hit me the first time he told me, "I'm
sorry, I'll never do it again."

This was repeated again, then the third time, and
he said the same exact thing, "Oh, it's because of
my drugs."

Then when he did it the last time I said to myself,
"There's not going to be another time. There's not
going to be a fifth time."

Belen, 17/Rafael, 17 (Travis, 3 months)

You may find yourself in a situation that you know is
wrong. If your partner hits you, you need to break away
from him, as was pointed out in the last chapter.

If Your Relationship Ends

All through this book we've been assuming that your
marriage, whether now or in the future, can last forever.
The underlying theme is the idea that if you and your partner work hard enough, if you trust, respect and care enough
for each other, you can have a satisfying life together.

While this is what most of us want when we marry,
reality for some couples is the knowledge that their

relationship isn't working. In fact, as mentioned before, the majority of teenage marriages fail within five years. Perhaps you and your spouse are sure your marriage isn't worth saving. What's the next step?

Good legal help is essential when you file for divorce. Costs of a lawyer's services vary tremendously.

Be as clear as possible about what you want from the lawyer before your first visit. The more visits, the more telephone calls, the more arguments to settle between you and your spouse, the more your lawyer will charge you.

If you don't have money to pay a lawyer, check with Legal Aid in your community. Another possibility is your local Bar Association. Call either one for advice on divorce procedures.

If you and your spouse don't have any children and no property to be divided, you may be granted a divorce quickly and simply. Each state sets up its own divorce laws, however. Check the law in your state.

In some states the husband and wife are jointly responsible for any debts incurred by either one until the day the divorce is final. The divorce settlement should be very specific as to who pays which debts.

Sometimes a woman is afraid of her ex-husband. Perhaps he's threatening that he will take their child away from her. He might become abusive if he sees her with another man.

She needs to understand that after her divorce is final, her former spouse has no rights over her. While he may have visitation rights with their child, only through court action "for good reason" could he have the custody agreement reversed.

If he is abusive or acts in an obnoxious manner toward her, she can get a restraining order from the police which should keep him away from her.

Grief of Divorce

Perhaps to your surprise, you feel sad after your divorce. You may be positive divorce is the best thing for you. Your marriage was a big mistake, and you're eager to get on with your life. Nevertheless, you're experiencing a loss, and grief is a natural response to a loss.

In the beginning, you probably thought your marriage would last forever. Even if losing your spouse at this point is a relief, you're still losing the idea and the hope that this marriage is going to work. There will be times when you'll feel sad or confused. You may wonder if you made the right decision. Carole had some of these feelings after she and Max were divorced:

> *It was such a traumatic thing to admit defeat, that it wasn't working. I hung on to that for a long time. It still is hard. I take it personally, and I have to talk myself out of it. I'd like to still be married and have a successful first marriage and have that go on forever.*
>
> *It's getting easier to where I can sit back and say, "Now wait a minute, don't start on this guilt trip."*

Divorce is seldom painless. If this happens to you, talking with friends may help. Or you may decide to see a good counselor.

If You Have a Child

The decision to divorce is even more difficult if you have a child. You may feel it's best for a child to have two parents, but you also know continuing a bad marriage only for the sake of the child is not likely to work well either for the parents or the child.

Mothers more often than fathers are awarded custody of their children. The court, however, no longer assumes the mother should have custody. The judge makes the decision, supposedly in the best interests of the child.

Generally if the father wants visitation rights, he will be granted those rights in the divorce decree. Child support payments, if any, will also be determined in the decree.

Sometimes divorced parents decide to co-parent their children. Each may have custody on alternate weeks, for example. This takes lots of cooperation, but in some cases is a good arrangement for the child. This setup usually works better if the parents live in the same area.

Even if you feel very negative about your child's other parent, be as positive as possible with your child. Saying the other parent is a no-good bum could make your child think she, too, is a no-good bum. You don't want that.

Whether or not you and your partner were married before you split, your joint responsibilities toward your child remain. Custody, visitation rights, and financial support remain the same whether or not you've ever been married.

When you marry again, of course your child will be involved in your plans. If he's beyond the infant stage, encourage him to talk about his feelings concerning the coming change in his life and yours.

Over and over young mothers, in speaking of a partner who is not their child's biological father, say, "He loves my child as if he were his own." And that is a reasonable goal. Rebecca wanted to make sure this would happen with Troy, 2, before she married again:

> *We lived together about four months before we got married. I never thought I would be one to just live with someone, but we moved in together as a prerequisite to marriage, not just for the heck of it. I knew I wanted to be married, but I also knew I couldn't have any kind of a marriage if either Don or Troy didn't like the other. This gave us all a chance to make sure marriage was right for us.*

Of course your new partner may have children, too.
Your children, my children, and our children offer some
real challenges to a relationship.

Should You Try Again?

Sometimes a divorced person wonders if s/he'll ever
have a happy marriage. Should you try again? Be assured
that if one marriage fails, it doesn't mean the next one will.

Some people, however, choose a second spouse remark-
ably like the first one. If her husband was an alcoholic, she
may marry another alcoholic. If his wife spent their money
foolishly, he may choose another spendthrift the second
time around.

If you want to make sure this doesn't happen to you,
think about the characteristics you disliked in your first
spouse. Think even more about the characteristics you'd
like in a partner. Your first marriage can teach you not only
what you don't want in a spouse, but also give you a clearer
idea of what you do want in your next relationship.

Include positive qualifications in your "What I want in
my next partner" list. You may not want someone who sits
in front of the TV all evening, but what do you want?
Someone who would enjoy sports with you? Someone who
will share your interest in music? Now is the time to think
about it.

A person who rushes into a second marriage soon after
ending the first may find earlier problems occurring again.
But if each takes the time to learn as much as possible
about the personality and values of the other before they
marry or move in together, their relationship is more likely
to last.

Divorce is difficult for everyone involved, but sometimes it's necessary. If this happens to you, get good legal
advice. Make loving and responsible arrangements for your
child. Then get on with your life. Good luck!

Spending time together is important.

CHAPTER 12

Leanne and Greg— Love and Caring

Leanne and Greg have been married 1 1/2 years. Their daughter, Natalie, is 20 months old. Like most young couples, Leanne and Greg have lived with in-laws, they have had money problems, they have dealt with changes when they married, they have arguments, they have faced early pregnancy and become parents together.

They share their budgeting techniques and early cooking, shopping, and cleaning efforts. They also talk about the importance of good communication and their ideas on keeping love alive. In fact, their story pretty much follows the topics of these chapters—and of the chapters in the companion volume, *Teenage Couples: Coping with Reality.*

Leanne and Greg have grown in their love for each other, and their relationship is satisfying to both of them.

Their story is included here as an illustration of the positive concepts in this book translated into real life.

Leanne Is Pregnant

Leanne: *We've been together almost four years. My pregnancy was a surprise. I was in tenth grade and Greg was a senior. Our families were disappointed, but they were supportive throughout the pregnancy and since.*

I grew up awfully fast, but I don't regret it. It helped that I stayed in school and was still around my friends. If I had dropped out, it would have been different. Then I would have had no contact with them at all.

Actually I've done better in school since I got pregnant. I told myself I'd be in school every day unless I was sick. Then after Natalie was born, I went every day unless she was sick and I had to stay home with her. I was determined. I didn't want to get bad grades and have to stay another year.

Some of the pregnant girls would miss a lot of school. They were just too tired to get up. I made myself get up. I said, "This is life. You have to deal with it. You can't feel sorry for yourself."

Greg: *When Leanne got pregnant, I felt overwhelmed. All of a sudden I had to be responsible—in an instant, and I mean the second I found out. It was a real eye-opener.*

I was a senior, and this changed my goals. I was going away to college and play my future by ear. Instead, I stayed here.

I was already working at a hardware store, and I'm still there. I started working when I was 15, partly because I didn't get an allowance. If I wanted to buy something, I had to earn it. So I started working just to get money for the things I wanted. I got my first car when I was 16.

My spending changed pretty quickly. Instead of buying CDs, I was buying diapers and paying hospital bills. I became more conservative in my buying.

When I found out that Leanne was pregnant, I pretty much cut off my free-spirited teen life. Leanne needed the support. I was lucky to have good friends who understood my position. I still got together with them, but not as much as before. It was disturbing at first, but I had to make that decision. It hurt, but not a lot.

The Marriage Decision

Leanne: *We waited until Natalie was two months old to get married. We weren't living together. We talked a lot about it. We didn't want to get married just because we had a baby. We wanted to make sure we loved each other.*

Greg was there a lot, especially after Natalie was born. He'd come by after work. Whatever free time he had after work, we'd do things together, usually with Natalie. Occasionally one of our parents would baby-sit.

Greg: *I changed my attitude during the time we were deciding whether to get married. When Leanne got pregnant, I did a lot of things that weren't in line. That was hard, but she straightened me out pretty good.*

When I was in high school, I partied a lot. That was pretty much all I did, and it caused a lot of conflict with Leanne. Partying was more important than doing stuff with her. She straightened me out.

That was a growing time for me because I was really irresponsible. I didn't have any cares. I was just out having a good time.

We decided we wanted to be committed to each other.

Living with Leanne's Mother

Leanne: *We lived with my mom for five months after we were married. When Greg moved in, we didn't have big complications. We were newlyweds, starting out as our own little family. We didn't have much privacy although we mostly stayed downstairs in the basement.*

It was actually nice because I was still in school, and my mom was able to help us out with the baby. So there was a positive and a negative side.

When you're young, you're all excited to get out on your own, but I'm glad we were able to stay with her a little while just to get on our feet.

My mom has always liked Greg. His family and I are close, too. My parents had liked Greg all along, and they placed no blame. It helps if the parents like the boyfriend before all this happens.

My mom did most of the cooking, but I'd help her. After Natalie was born, I think my mom did more around the house. I had a baby to take care of, but I still tried to keep up my end of the stick.

Greg: *Living with Leanne's mom those first five months was a load off my shoulders because I didn't have to pay rent. We also didn't have to make the meals during that time. It was still a lot of responsibility, but we could sort of edge into it instead of being overwhelmed with everything at once.*

We pretty much dominated the basement. It was

like a little apartment. Leanne's mom worked. When she was home, she didn't feel she had to sit with us and watch TV. She let us live our own lives.

Planning the Spending

Leanne: *Of course money was a problem. When we were living with my mom, we helped pay the bills. We had to budget our money. Greg's dad talked to us and showed us a basic budget plan. He helped us plan. It's a lot less stressful when you know how you're going to spend your money, and you aren't just buying things here and there, wasting it.*

We figured out the amount of money we needed for rent, medical, car, etc. We hadn't paid those bills in the past, and he helped us get an idea of what to expect. We learned a lot about money management those five months we spent with my mom.

I was on my dad's insurance so that paid for the hospital bills for me and Natalie. That was great. We have family insurance now through Greg's work.

We knew when we moved into our apartment that we'd really have to stretch to make ends meet. It's amazing how fast your money disappears into bills and rent.

We usually agree on how we spend it. If there's something we want or need, we usually ask each other and see where we'll go with our money. We save money each month.

Greg: *Managing our money is a matter of survival. It's something we have to do to make it day to day. Sure, Leanne sees a nice dress she wants, or I see an amplifier for my guitar—but there are other things that are more important. You just have to get your priorities straight.*

My dad helped us a lot. He told us to lay it out on paper, the money we'd have, and the bills we'd have. We did that, and he looked at it. He suggested we adjust a little here and there, then go ahead and try it out. Being on a budget makes a big difference. You know where your money is going, and you can plan accordingly. It takes off some of the stress.

My job situation looks pretty good. My manager suggested some courses to take at the community college to educate me for a management position. So I'm doing that now. Leanne is also taking a college class.

We can't justify Leanne going to work to pay for day care. She wants to go back to work after Natalie is in school and after our second child is in school. She'll work full-time then.

Handling Apartment Living

Leanne: *It was hard when we moved into our apartment. When I was in school I usually left our laundry for the weekend. When you have a baby, the laundry builds up fast.*

Then the cleaning. We try to pick up nights before we go to bed. I usually leave the cleaning for Saturday. Greg helps me although I do most of it now that I'm out of school and he's working full-time. I don't mind.

I'm a little more picky about neatness than Greg is. It's hard trying to keep a house picked up, especially with a little one. We don't mind the toys around, but when I have to pick up his socks, it gets frustrating. My main gripe is when he leaves clothes lying around on the bedroom floor, and the clothes basket is just a few feet away. It bothers me. I remind him where the clothes basket is.

*It bothers me when Greg drinks out of the milk jug.
Natalie likes to play with the empty milk carton, and
sometimes I see her tipping it up just like her dad.*

Greg: *When Leanne was in school, whoever had
the time did the cleaning. Now, if I come home real
tired, I'm not usually inspired to vacuum the carpet.*

Learning to Cook and Shop

Leanne: *Greg is a good cook although I do most of
it. We both like to try new foods so I experiment out of
cookbooks, get new ideas. It gets boring to eat the
same kind of foods, so we fix a variety. Some evenings
it's as simple as grilled cheese sandwiches.*

*I do the grocery shopping. I usually plan meals and
make a list. Sometimes I ask Greg what he'd like this
week. Or I'll thumb through a cookbook for ideas. We
like pasta and we like Mexican food.*

*If I don't make a list, my mind goes blank when I
go into the grocery store. And if I don't have a list,
I'll think, this looks good, I'll buy that. Then I end up
spending more money than I need to.*

*I try to shop about twice a week. We have noticed
that if I go more often, I spend more money. I read
food ads. I use coupons and get things on sale. I
learned all this from my mom. She has always
done this.*

*I also read magazines and use some of those
recipes. When you first start out, it's hard to get
ideas. It was awful because I could think of only a few
things to cook.*

*I wasn't especially concerned with nutrition until
Natalie started eating real food. I try to cook foods
she can eat, fix a meal that has everything for her*

*because she's a growing little girl. That helps Greg
and me eat healthy.*

Greg: *Tonight I made sautéed mushrooms with
steak. I was telling Leanne how glad I am she likes
mushrooms. I can't imagine anyone not liking
mushrooms.*

Communication Tips

Leanne: *When we disagree, Greg usually likes to
kind of wait to talk about it. He's a real calm person,
and I blow up at things more easily. I'm usually the
one that gets upset.*

*It's important to be open with each other. Commu-
nication helps a relationship. It can be hard if you
don't have an open mind, or the other person doesn't
want to consider your feelings.*

Greg: *We communicate pretty well. I was real
lacking in that department, especially if I didn't like
something. I'd just shrug it off. I really had to work
on that. Leanne communicates real well, and she
helped me learn to communicate better.*

*If we're upset with each other, we talk about it
before we go to sleep. It's a quiet time when Natalie
is sleeping and there aren't other distractions. We
talk about it, analyze the problem, and figure out
what we can do to fix it.*

Keeping Love Alive

Leanne: *We spend much of our free time together.
There's no jealousy that I've ever noticed. When we
were in high school, we had a lot of friends, male and
female, and I got to know his friends. He's a real
friendly, open guy, and I've never been jealous. I*

know his personality, and I know almost everybody
likes him, so I've never had any jealousy. We both
had boy and girl friends.

There never was any hitting. You want to stay away
from abusive relationships. I think you have to look at
their family ties. That's a big part of it. If their parents are alcoholic or abusive, it can carry through to
their children.

Sometimes we go to the movies. We go camping.
Our parents take care of Natalie occasionally, and we
like to do a lot of things with our friends—go bowling,
have them over here, play games. We do a lot of that,
especially with two friends who got married last year
and have a child.

Most of my friends stuck with me throughout my
pregnancy. After I got married and the baby was
older, some no longer called me to go to the mall or
whatever. But I notice the friends I've had the longest
stick by me. They still come over. We still do things
when I'm available.

Greg and I agree that we both need our own lives.
When we have free time, he and his friends work on
their stereo equipment together or go skiing. Me and
my girlfriends go shopping. You need to have your
own life apart, too.

Especially when you have children, you need to
make time for each other. We both have busy schedules. Once Greg gets home and we have dinner, our
evenings go by so quick. Some nights we just plop
ourselves down in front of the TV, and I think that's
what a lot of people do, just turn on the tube. You
need to make time for each other, shut off everything
and talk.

There's a lot of work in a good relationship.

Greg: *Like Leanne said, we have separate interests. After work three days a week, I work out for two
hours. That gives me a chance to get things off my
mind. Pump some iron and burn some energy.*

*I like music. I play the bass. I like different kinds of
music and Leanne likes crafts.*

*I think Natalie strengthened our relationship. We
laugh a lot more. I'm pretty involved with her. I see
her in the morning before I go to work, and I come
home for lunch and see her.*

We go out together. We enjoy our time together.

When asked for advice for other couples, Greg replied:

*Mainly to be committed to each other. If you're
going to do this together, you might as well do it all
the way. Don't give just half of yourself. Give all of
yourself to your spouse and your child, and I think
everything else kind of falls into place.*

May **your** relationship, like Leanne and Greg's, grow
and develop into an ever more caring and loving
partnership.

APPENDIX

Predicting Success of Teenage Marriage

Love, based on trust, respect, and caring, is the most important ingredient of a good marriage, but it is impossible to measure these very special ingredients. Other important factors in developing a lasting marriage can be measured, however.

The following questions are designed to measure your partner's and your readiness for marriage. Your score can give you a rough estimate of your chances for a successful marriage. Answer the following questions *honestly* by circling the number (1, 2, 3, 4 or 5) of your answer—or write the numbers on another sheet of paper. Then ask your partner to answer the questions. Do your scores match?

1. How old are you?
   1. 16   **2.** 17   **3.** 18   **4.** 19   **5.** 20 or older

2. How old is your partner?
   1. 16   **2.** 17   **3.** 18   **4.** 19   **5.** 20 or older

3. What is the highest grade in school you have completed?
   1. Grade 10   **2.** Grade 11   **3.** Grade 12 **4.** Grade 13   **5.** Grade 14

4. What is the highest grade in school your partner completed?
   1. Grade 10   **2.** Grade 11   **3.** Grade 12 **4.** Grade 13   **5.** Grade 14

5. Do you and your partner belong to the same ethnic group?
   3. No   **5.** Yes

6. Do you and your partner agree on religion?
   1. Disagree completely   **2.** Disagree somewhat
   3. It's not important to us   **4.** Mostly agree   **5.** Agree completely

7. Are your family backgrounds pretty much alike?
   1. Not at all   **3.** Somewhat alike   **5.** Very much alike

8. On a scale of 1 to 5, how good do you feel about yourself?
   Not good at all—**1**—**2**—**3**—**4**—**5**—Very good (high self-esteem)

9. On a scale of 1 to 5, how good does your partner feel about him/herself?
   Not good at all—**1**—**2**—**3**—**4**—**5**—Very good (high self-esteem)

10. How long have you known each other?
    1. 1-3 months   **2.** 3-6 months   **3.** 6-12 months
    4. 12-18 months   **5.** 18 months or more

11. Are you (or is your partner) pregnant?   **2.** Yes   **5.** No

12. On a scale of 1 to 5, how well do you and your partner agree on how many children you want and if/when you want them?
    Don't agree at all—**1**—**2**—**3**—**4**—**5**—Agree perfectly

13. How do you feel about your partner's parents?
    I don't like them at all—**1**—**2**—**3**—**4**—**5**—I think they're wonderful

14. Is either of you marrying to escape a bad family situation?
    1. Yes   **5.** No

16. Does either of you think the other one has a drug or alcohol problem?   **1.** Yes   **5.** No

17. How jealous are you and your partner of each other?
    Terribly jealous—**1**—**2**—**3**—**4**—**5**—We trust each other completely

18. How much do you and your partner argue?

    1. Constantly   **3.** Never   **5.** Occasionally

19. How many interests and activities do you share with your partner?

    1. One   **2.** Two   **3.** Three   **4.** Four   **5.** Five or more

20. Does either or both of you have a good job now?

    1. Neither one   **2.** No, but one is in school

    3. No, but both are in school   **4.** Yes, one of us   **5.** Yes, both of us

21. On a scale of 1 to 5, how well do you and your partner agree on how you spend your money?

    We don't agree at all—**1**—**2**—**3**—**4**—**5**—We almost always agree

22. How do you and your partner feel about traditional versus equal marriage as defined in Chapter 3?

    1. We don't agree   **3.** We both want a traditional marriage

    5. We both want an equal marriage

23. On a scale of 1 to 5, how well do you and your partner communicate with each other?

    Poorly—**1**—**2**—**3**—**4**—**5**—Very well

Now total your score. If it's between 100 and 115, you and your partner have a lot going for you. Good luck!

If you score 90-99, be careful. You're likely to have a rough time if you get married or move in together now.

Is your score between 70 and 79? How about postponing your marriage or living-together decision for at least a year?

If you score below 70, you two don't appear to have much going for you. Please consider looking for someone else—or at least postponing your decision for quite a while.

Of course there is no measure that will guarantee either a happy relationship or a bad one. This scorecard is designed simply to help you and your partner consider some crucial factors involved in making perhaps the most important decision of your life. Please think carefully!

Description of Interviewees

Sometimes a problem becomes easier to deal with if you know you aren't the only one with such a problem. Hearing someone else talk about feelings of jealousy, for example, may help you look more realistically at your own situation.

This book and its companion title, *Teenage Couples—Coping with Reality: Dealing with Money, In-Laws, Babies and Other Details of Daily Life,* are based on information, opinions, and suggestions from 80 young people I interviewed extensively. Each was living or had lived with a partner.

Thirty-one of the interviewees were married, and for 13 couples, both husband and wife were interviewed.

Of the 31 married interviewees, 18 did not live together before they were married while 13 did.

Twelve of the interviewees were no longer living with

their partner, although three were still "together."

Sixty-five of the 80 interviewees had lived together with his parents or hers. Half of the total group were still with parents at the time of the interview, while 40 were living by themselves at that time.

Almost half of the interviewees (39) were living in California. Other states represented by interviewees included Florida, Georgia, Pennsylvania, Ohio, Illinois, Nebraska, Montana, and Oregon.

Interviewee Data							
Sex		**Male** 26			**Female** 54		
Age **14**	**15**	**16**	**17**	**18**	**19**	**20**	**21+**
1	3	11	19	19	8	7	12
Note: All were living with a partner before age 20 or, if older, lived with a partner younger than 20.							
Lived together		≤1 yr. 25		1-2 yr. 36		2-3 yr. 12	3+ yr. 7
Married?		**Yes** 29			**No** 51		
Ethnic **Group**	**Hispanic** 28	**White** 30		**Black** 12	**Native Am** 7		**Asian** 3
Number of **Children**	**None** 4	**Pregnant** 7		**1** 58	**2** 10		**3** 1

Description
of Survey Respondents

The Marriage Expectations Survey mentioned occasionally in both *Teenage Couples* books was developed in order to obtain current information concerning teens' attitudes toward marriage and other long-term relationships.

Two questionnaires were utilized, one for those teens not yet married or living with a partner, and the other for teens already in such a relationship. Teachers administering the survey had both questionnaires in quantities as needed.

While the questionnaires were similar, the first focused on respondents' expectations for their future marriage or living-together arrangements. Included were questions such as "How much do you think getting married or living with a partner at age 18 or younger would change your life . . . ?" and "If/when you marry or live with a partner, who should be responsible for preparing meals?"

The questionnaire for those already living with a partner placed more emphasis on the realities of the respondents, as "How much has getting married or living with your partner changed your life . . .?" and "In *your* relationship, who is mostly responsible for preparing meals?"

A total of 3728 young people completed the questionnaires. Nearly all were in school, and the questionnaires were administered by their teachers, most often in a home economics class.

Six hundred seventy of the respondents were living with or had lived with a partner, so completed the Living Together (LT) questionnaire.The others, 3,058, responded to the other questionnaire.

Nearly half of the Living-Together group were attending a comprehensive high school or junior high, and almost as many were attending a special school for pregnant and parenting teens or another alternative school. Of the larger group (those not living with a partner), 12 percent were in a special school while nearly all the others were in high school or junior high.

Students from forty-nine states responded to the Not-Living-Together questionnaire. (Results from an Idaho school were lost en route.) Forty-three states were represented by the Living-Together sample.

See the next page for biographical data covering both groups.

For a questionnaire much like those used in the survey, but minus the biographical data, see pages 171-180 of *Teenage Couples—Coping with Reality.*

A detailed analysis of the results of these surveys is titled *Teenage Couples—Rainbows, Roles and Reality: A Comparison of Teens' Expectations of Marriage with the Realities of Those Already Living Together* (Morning Glory Press).

Survey Respondent Data

Sex	Female	Male
Not living together (NLT)	2,297	761
Living together (LT)	601	69

Age	12	13	14	15	16	17	18	19	20+
NLT	46	92	287	517	728	866	419	69	26
LT	1	10	49	121	232	177	55	25	

Ethnic Group	His-panic	White	African Amer.	Native Amer.	Asian	Mixed
NLT	346	1,302	676	372	31	277
LT	213	227	71	67	13	62

Religion	Catholic	Protestant	Born-Again Christian	Jewish
NLT	796	398	484	14
LT	218	47	91	1

	Muslim	Other	No Religious Affiliation
NLT	28	782	518
LT	2	136	166

Females: Ever been pregnant?	Never	Pregnant Now	Mis-carried	Abor-tion	Adop-tion	Have Child
NLT	1,486	308	88	48	6	396
LT	65	194	36	19	4	339

Males: Ever gotten a woman pregnant?	No	Yes, one	Yes, two or more	I don't know
NLT	516	60	31	66
LT	20	30	8	6

ANNOTATED BIBLIOGRAPHY

Many books are available in which marriage in general is discussed. Several hundred titles are listed under "Marriage" in the current edition of *Books in Print*. Quite a few resources concerned with teenage pregnancy and parenthood have been published. However, there are very few books dealing directly with teenage marriage. In fact, the same edition of *Books in Print* lists only two under "Teenage Marriage."

The following bibliography includes the books mentioned in *Teenage Couples: Caring, Commitment and Change*. Also listed are some additional titles on relationship building plus a novel with this theme. Easy readability, high interest level, and practicality of information were the major criteria for selection of titles.

Prices quotes are from *Books in Print*, 1994. Because prices change so rapidly, however, and because publishers move, it is wise to call your local library reference department for an updated price and address before ordering a book. If you can't find a book you want in your bookstore, you can usually get it directly from the publisher. Enclose $2.50 for shipping in addition to the price of the book. See page 208 for an order form for Morning Glory Press publications.

Ayer, Eleanor H. *Everything You Need to Know About Teen Marriage.* 1991. 64 pp. $13.95. The Rosen Publishing Group, Inc., 29 East 21st Street, New York City, NY 10010. 800/237-9932.
From the Need to Know Library, this is a brief but rather comprehensive overview of teenage marriage.

Bessell, Harold, Ph.D. *Romance with the Right Person: A Guide to Understanding True Love.* 1993. 147 pp. $9.95. New Horizon Books, P.O. Box 226, Poway, CA 92064. 619/486-3404.
Goal of the book is to give young people the essential skills they need to find, recognize, and maintain healthy love relationships. Simple questionnaire format.

Colgrove, Melba, Harold Bloomfield, and Peter McWilliam. *How to Survive the Loss of a Love.* 1991. $10. Prelude Press, 8159 Santa Monica Boulevard, Los Angeles, CA 90046. 800/543-3101.
Daily affirmations, survival poems, and sayings for anyone who has lost someone special.

"Dating Violence! Cara and Kevin Talk to Teens" and **"Date Rape! Terri and J.R. Talk to Teens."** 1990. Leaflets. 50/$15; Quantity discounts. ETR Associates, P.O. Box 1830, Santa Cruz, CA 95061-1830. 800/321-4407.
*Great resources. "Dating Violence," especially, should be required reading for **all** teenagers and preteens—and for older people who still think violence in a relationship is either okay or a fact of life.*

DeVault, Christine. **Sexuality Decision-Making Series for Teens:** *Too Soon for Sex?; Taking Chances with Sex; Don't Let It Get Around.* 1990. 119, 163, 166 pp. $3.95 each. 25+/$3.50 each. **Teaching Ideas for Using the Sexuality Decision-Making Books for Teens** by Kathleen Middleton. 1990. 23 pp. $3.95. ETR Associates, P.O. Box 1830, Santa Cruz, CA 95061-1830. 800/321-4407.
Each story changes depending on the reader's choices, helping teens build the social and cognitive skills they need to make healthy decisions about sexual involvement. Good for role playing.

Gale, Jay, and Sheila Church. *30 Days to a Happier Marriage.* 1992, 183 pp. Hardcover, $15.95. Longmeadow Press, 201 High Ridge Road, Stamford, CT 06904. 203/352-2110.
Simple lessons that can help you build a stronger, more stimulating relationship. Stresses learning to communicate more effectively.

Gottman, John, Ph.D. *Why Marriages Succeed or Fail.* 1994, 234 pp. Hardcover, $21. Simon & Schuster, Rockefeller Center, 1230 Avenue of the Americas, New York, NY 10020. 212/698-7000.
A practical guide to repairing the way wives and husbands relate to each other and removing the patterns that lead to divorce.

Gordon, Sol. *Why Love Is Not Enough.* 1990. 153 pp. $6.95. Bob Adams, Inc., 260 Center Street, Holbrook, MA 02343-1074. 800/872-5627.
Offers practical advice on relationship building. A good book for teens ready to consider mature versus immature relationships. Portions could provide excellent material for class discussions.

_____. *"Is There Anything I Can Do?" Helping a Friend When Times Are Tough.* 1994. 220 pp. Hardcover, $21.95. Delacorte Press, 1540 Broadway, New York, NY 10036. 800/221-4676.
Another excellent book from Sol Gordon. It's not about living with a partner, but it provides valuable suggestions for being a good friend— invaluable in a partnership.

Head, Ann. *Mr. and Mrs. Bo Jo Jones.* 1973. $3.99. Signet. NAL/ Dutton. 375 Hudson Street, New York, NY 10014-3657. 212/366-2000.
This story of a 16-year-old bride and 17-year-old groom who married because of pregnancy is still in print. It's an all-time favorite of teenagers.

Kilgore, Nancy. *Every Eighteen Seconds: A Journey Through Domestic Violence.* 1993. 109 pp. $8.95. Volcano Press, Inc., P.O. Box 270-E, Volcano, CA 95689-0270. 209/296-3445.
With sensitivity and honesty, this story of one woman's escape from her battering husband encourages others to move on to better lives.

Kiner, Dr. Melvyn, and Dr. Connell Cowan. *Husbands and Wives: The Guide for Men and Women Who Want to Stay Married.* 1989. 317 pp. $4.95. Signet, NAL/Dutton, 375 Hudson Street, New York, NY 10014. 212/366-2000.
The authors, through a discussion of self-directed marriage, offer real help in establishing renewed love and intimacy.

Lansky, Vickie. *Getting Your Child to Sleep . . . and Back to Sleep.* 1991. 132 pp. $6.95. The Book Peddlers, 18326 Minnetonka Boulevard, Deephaven, MN 55391. 612/475-3527.

Book offers a wealth of suggestions for dealing with babies and small children who don't sleep as regularly as their parents would like.

Leman, Dr. Kevin. ***Sex Begins in the Kitchen—Renewing Emotional and Physical Intimacy in Marriage.*** 1992. $8. Dell Publishing Co., 1540 Broadway, New York, NY 10036-4094. 800/223-6834.
While Dr. Leman is not writing specifically to teenage couples, his book is a wonderful resource for couples of any age. It's interesting and easy to read. His point that sex is an all-day affair based on the couple's total relationship is an important concept. He uses lots of examples from his experience as a marriage and family counselor and in presenting Family Living Seminars throughout the country. His writing style is witty. It's a delightful book.

Lindsay, Jeanne Warren. ***Teenage Couples—Coping with Reality: Dealing with Money, In-laws, Babies and Other Details of Daily Life.*** 1995. 192 pp. Paper, $9.95; hardcover, $15.95. Workbook, $2.50. Curriculum Guide (includes ***Teenage Couples—Caring, Commitment and Change)***, $19.95. Morning Glory Press, 6595 San Haroldo Way, Buena Park, CA 90620. 714/828-1998.
*Companion volume to **Teenage Couples—Caring, Commitment and Change**. Good discussion, as the title implies, of the financial responsibilities of marriage and living together, living with in-laws, importance of education, role-sharing, pregnancy, and parenting. Lots of quotes from teenage couples.*

Matiella, Ana Consuelo. ***Saturday Night Special: A Story of Choices.*** 1989. 27 pp. photonovella. $1.50; 50/$50; 200/$150. ETR Associates, P.O. Box 1830, Santa Cruz, CA 95061-1830. 800/321-4407.
Wonderful booklet. Two couples move from an "I can't talk about it" mind set to being able to discuss their need for mutual protection from AIDS.

Marecek, Mary. ***Breaking Free from Partner Abuse.*** 1993. 64 pp. $7.95. Quantity discount. Morning Glory Press, 6595 San Haroldo Way, Buena Park, CA 90620. 714/828-1998.
Lovely illustrations by Jami Moffett. Underlying message is that the reader does not deserve to be hit. Simply written. Can help a young woman escape an abusive relationship.

McCoy, Kathy, and Charles Wibbelsman, M.D. ***The New Teenage Body Book Guide.*** 1992. $14.95. Putnam Publishing Group, 200 Madison Avenue, New York, NY 10016. 800/631-8571.

The book is crammed with information for teenagers about everything from their bodies, changing feelings, teenage beauty, and special medical needs of young adults to sexuality, venereal disease, birth control, pregnancy and parenthood. It is written directly to teenagers with lots of quotes from young people, sometimes in the form of questions, in each chapter.

Nelson-Kilger, Shirley, Josefina J. Card, and James L. Peterson. 1990. ***Letters to Dr. Know: Letters and Answers About Teenage Sexuality and Pregnancy.*** 1990. 156 pp. $15. Sociometrics Corporation, 170 State Street, Suite 260, Los Altos, CA 94022-2812. 415/949-3282.

Seventy-five letters from teens with questions about sexuality are answered wisely, compassionately, and with some humor. Also available in computer version, "Ask Dr. Know" (also $15), which utilizes vivid sound and graphics.

"Nobody's Fool Again: Three Teens Talk About Being Mothers." "Time Out: Three Guys Take Time Out to Discuss Sex, Pregnancy, and Relationships." 6 pp. each. 1-49/30¢ each; 50+/25¢ each plus 15% shpg. Planned Parenthood of Summit, Portage and Medina Counties, 34 South High Street, Akron, OH 44308. 216/535-2674.

*Both pamphlets include photos and entertaining accounts of young people's lives. Boys and girls would gain increased understanding of themselves and their partners by reading **both** pamphlets.*

Walker, Lenore. ***The Battered Woman.*** 1982. 224 pp. Paper, $11. HarperCollins, 10 E. 53rd Street, New York, NY 10022. 800/331-3761.

At least half the women in the United States are hit by their husbands or boyfriends at some time, according to Ms. Walker. Her book contains many disturbing case studies. It also includes sections on preventive education, practical remedies including shelters, and a discussion of psychotherapy.

Weeks, John R. ***Teenage Marriages—A Demographic Analysis.*** 1976. $45. Greenwood Press, 88 Post Rd. W., Westport, CT 06881. *Old research, but still the only such study listed in **Books in Print**. This is a detailed report of a study started in 1970 as part of a larger program of investigation into fertility and family formation at International Population and Urban Research (IPUR), University of California, Berkeley. It's a good discussion of teenage marriage in the United States including lots of statistics through 1973.*

ABOUT THE AUTHOR

Jeanne Warren Lindsay has worked with hundreds of pregnant and parenting teenagers. She developed the Teen Parent Program at Tracy

High School, Cerritos, California, in 1972, and coordinated the program for many years. She is the author of 15 other books dealing with adolescent pregnancy and parenting. Her *Teens Parenting* four-book series and *Teen Dads: Rights, Responsibilities and Joys* are widely used with pregnant and parenting teens.

Jeanne has graduate degrees in Anthropology and Home Economics. She and Bob have five children and five grandchildren.

ABOUT THE PHOTOGRAPHER

David Crawford, M.A., has been a photographer and counselor to pregnant and parenting teens for more than 25 years in the Elk Grove

Unified School District, Sacramento, California, where he co-directs the Program for Pregnant and Parenting Students. His quiet fatherly image has been a settling force in the personal lives of many of his students and their families. David teaches prenatal care, parenting, and photography, blending education and training to enhance his students' confidence and self-esteem.

David and Peggy have a son, Alton, 24, and have co-parented several other children. He is godfather to many others.

OTHER RESOURCES FROM MORNING GLORY PRESS

TEENAGE COUPLES—Caring, Commitment and Change: How to Build a Relationship that Lasts. TEENAGE COUPLES— Coping with Reality: Dealing with Money, In-Laws, Babies and Other Details of Daily Life. Two books to help teenage couples develop healthy, loving and lasting relationships.

TEENS PARENTING—Your Pregnancy and Newborn Journey How to take care of yourself and your newborn. For pregnant teens. Available in "regular" (RL 6), Easier Reading (RL 3), and Spanish.

TEENS PARENTING—Your Baby's First Year
TEENS PARENTING—The Challenge of Toddlers
TEENS PARENTING—Discipline from Birth to Three
Three how-to-parent books especially for teenage parents.

VIDEO: "Discipline from Birth to Three" supplements above book.

TEEN DADS: Rights, Responsibilities and Joys. Parenting book for teenage fathers.

DETOUR FOR EMMY. Novel about teenage pregnancy.

TOO SOON FOR JEFF. Novel from teen father's perspective.

SURVIVING TEEN PREGNANCY: Choices, Dreams, Decisions For all pregnant teens—help with decisions, moving on toward goals.

SCHOOL-AGE PARENTS: The Challenge of Three-Generation Living. Help for families when teen daughter (or son) has a child.

BREAKING FREE FROM PARTNER ABUSE. Guidance for victims of domestic violence.

DID MY FIRST MOTHER LOVE ME? A Story for an Adopted Child. Birthmother shares her reasons for placing her child.

DO I HAVE A DADDY? A Story About a Single-Parent Child Picture/story book especially for children with only one parent. Also available in Spanish, *¿Yo tengo papá?*

OPEN ADOPTION: A Caring Option A fascinating and sensitive account of the new world of adoption.

PARENTS, PREGNANT TEENS AND THE ADOPTION OPTION. For parents of teens considering an adoption plan..

PREGNANT TOO SOON: Adoption Is an Option. Written to pregnant teens who may be considering an adoption plan.

ADOPTION AWARENESS: A Guide for Teachers, Counselors, Nurses and Caring Others. How to talk about adoption when no one is interested.

TEEN PREGNANCY CHALLENGE, Book One: Strategies for Change; Book Two: Programs for Kids. Practical guidelines for developing adolescent pregnancy prevention and care programs.

MORNING GLORY PRESS

6595 San Haroldo Way, Buena Park, CA 90620
714/828-1998 — FAX 714/828-2049

Please send me the following: Price   Total

Teenage Couples: Caring, Commitment and Change
—   Paper, 0-930934-93-8   9.95 ————
—   Cloth, ISBN 0-930934-92-x   15.95 ————
    Teenage Couples: Coping with Reality
—   Paper, ISBN 0-930934-86-5   9.95 ————
—   Cloth, ISBN 0-930934-87-3   15.95 ————
— ***Too Soon for Jeff***   Paper, ISBN 0-930934-91-1   8.95 ————
—   Cloth, ISBN 0-930934-90-3   15.95 ————
—***Detour for Emmy***   Paper, ISBN 0-930934-76-8   8.95 ————
—   Cloth, ISBN 0-930934-75-x   15.95 ————
—***Teen Dads***   Paper, ISBN 0-930934-78-4   9.95 ————
—   Cloth, ISBN 0-930934-77-6   15.95 ————
—***Do I Have a Daddy?***   Cloth, ISBN 0-930934-45-8   12.95 ————
—***Did My First Mother Love Me?*** ISBN 0-930934-85-7   12.95 ————
—***Breaking Free from Partner Abuse*** 0-930934-74-1 $7.95 ————
—***Surviving Teen Pregnancy*** Paper, 0-930934-47-4 $9.95 ————
    School-Age Parents: Three-Generation Living
—   Paper, ISBN 0-930934-36-9   10.95 ————
   Teens Parenting—Your Pregnancy and Newborn Journey
—   Paper, ISBN 0-930934-50-4   9.95 ————
—   Cloth, ISBN 0-930934-51-2   15.95 ————
   Easier Reading Edition—*Pregnancy and Newborn Journey*
—   Paper, ISBN 0-930934-61-x   9.95 ————
—   Cloth, ISBN 0-930934-62-8   15.95 ————
   Spanish—Adolescentes como padres—La jornada . . .
—   Paper, ISBN 0-930934-69-5   9.95 ————
   Teens Parenting—Your Baby's First Year
—   Paper, ISBN 0-930934-52-0   9.95 ————
—   Cloth, ISBN 0-930934-53-9   15.95 ————
   Teens Parenting—Challenge of Toddlers
—   Paper, ISBN 0-930934-58-x   9.95 ————
—   Cloth, ISBN 0-930934-59-8   15.95 ————
   Teens Parenting—Discipline from Birth to Three
—   Paper, ISBN 0-930934-54-7   9.95 ————
—   Cloth, ISBN 0-930934-55-5   15.95 ————
—**VIDEO:** "Discipline from Birth to Three"   195.00 ————

                              TOTAL   ————

Please add postage: 10% of total—Min., $2.50   ————
California residents add 7.75% sales tax   ————
                           TOTAL   ————

Ask about quantity discounts, Teacher, Student Guides.
Prepayment requested. School/library purchase orders accepted.
If not satisfied, return in 15 days for refund.

NAME ————————————————————————

ADDRESS ——————————————————————